Artificial Intelligence, ESG Investments and the Future of Tokenized Assets

Artificial Intelligence, ESG Investments and the Future of Tokenized Assets

BY

SEAN STEIN SMITH
City University of New York, USA

emerald PUBLISHING

United Kingdom – North America – Japan – India – Malaysia – China

Emerald Publishing Limited
Emerald Publishing, Floor 5, Northspring, 21-23 Wellington Street, Leeds LS1 4DL.

First edition 2026

British Library Cataloguing in Publication Data
A catalogue record for this book is available from the British Library

ISBN: 978-1-83708-109-7 (Print)
ISBN: 978-1-83708-108-0 (Online)
ISBN: 978-1-83708-110-3 (Epub)

Printed and bound by CPI Group (UK) Ltd, Croydon, CR0 4YY

This book is dedicated to family, for their continuous support of my ideas, ambitions, and goals.

Contents

Chapter 1

Introduction

Abstract

The accelerating convergence of artificial intelligence (AI); environmental, social, and governance (ESG) priorities; and tokenized assets is reshaping the business and financial landscape. This text explores how generative AI (GenAI) is transforming decision-making, ESG remains a critical – though politicized – driver of investment and governance, and tokenized assets are gaining traction across traditional finance. Simultaneously, private equity (PE) is reshaping accounting firms, driving technology adoption, and altering firm structures. Government efforts, led by DOGE, are scrutinizing public consulting contracts, impacting major firms like Deloitte. As these trends converge, financial professionals must stay informed to navigate new opportunities, risks, and evolving market expectations.

Keywords: Artificial intelligence; environmental, social, and governance; tokenized assets; private equity in accounting; government efficiency; blockchain and cryptoassets

The business landscape continues to shift and evolve at an accelerating pace and several of the fundamental trends driving this change are AI, ESG reporting and information, as well as the proliferation of cryptoassets throughout the financial landscape. While these technologies and reporting paradigms have evolved in distinct manners and have been adopted by different firms in the marketplace, the reality is that these three areas are growing and influencing each other simultaneously. Separately, these trends would be sufficient to disrupt business and the status quo but since these converging trends are developing at the same time, and attracting billions in investments, financial practitioners must be informed about these tools as well as how these tools are changing the business decision-making process. To that end, it seems reasonable to level set and introduce these topics.

Artificial Intelligence, ESG Investments and the Future of Tokenized Assets, 1–9

Published under exclusive licence by Emerald Publishing Limited
doi:10.1108/978-1-83708-108-020261001

AI first bursts into the mainstream conversation in December 2022 with the launch of ChatGPT 3.5, the flagship product developed by OpenAI. Following the launch of ChatGPT, the mass market appeal and use cases for AI became clear across industry lines. At the time of launch, the subsequent improvements to the AI program that have been released subsequently have further spurred investments and adoption of AI by firms across economic lines. In addition to the trends, adoption, and investment of AI directly, the AI boom has also powered growth and earnings in companies such as Nvidia that are supplying the majority of chips used by AI programs. To put into bluntly, AI and other software applications are continuing to attract the majority of investments and investor attention at the expense of virtually all other tools and applications.

For the purposes of this text, the subset of AI that will be focused on will be GenAI, as this type of AI represents the aspect of AI that has taken the marketplace by storm since launch. Colloquially, GenAI can be thought of as the "killer app" that many emerging technologies seek but relatively few are able to achieve in most market conditions. Especially since GenAI has proven itself exceptionally capable at digesting large amounts of information, working and collaborating with human counterparts, and creating new forms of content and information, the implications of these tools look set to continue expanding.

ESG as an investment theme might seem like a relatively new trend, but it is actually an outgrowth of previous trends and pivots that have changed the investing and societal landscape in both the United States and internationally (Comoli et al., 2023). As an increasing amount of interest and investment has been allocated into these areas, the importance of financial statement reporting, standardizing ESG reporting, and updating governance protocols is directly influencing accounting standards and standard setting (Choi & Lee, 2024). Although this investment trend has unfortunately become politicized in the post-2020 era, the fact remains that the elements of ESG will continue to play an important role in how organizations plan investment and strategic activities. In addition, it will have an outsized role in the talent acquisition and retention strategies of firms for the foreseeable future. Let's take a moment and provide brief working definitions for each of the components of ESG.

Environmental. The environmental aspect of ESG reporting and information is perhaps the subset most easily understood, with individuals and institutions seeking to reduce environmental effects of operations while pursuing greener options.

Social / societal. The social angle involved in ESG reporting is simultaneously the most ambiguous but can also be the most challenging to quantify. For the purposes of introduction, let's summarize the societal aspect as organizations being aware of both the clients and communities they serve.

Governance. In the age of advancing AI, and as AI applications continue to accelerate the collective ability to learn, reason, and evolve the ability of firms to govern and establish governance protocols will only increase in importance over time. Specifically, governance relates to the ability of the firm to navigate changing market conditions driving change and disruption from both inside the firm and outside of the firm.

Although the benefits of a stakeholder model of enterprise management have been discussed at length for decades, the recent pivot toward ESG investment and asset management has unfortunately also become associated with political trends and opinions. Regardless of this, the further refinement of ESG accounting is rapidly pivoting from an optional field of study to one that is increasingly seen as necessary from both a conceptual and applied perspective (Lorne & Li, 2024). As usually occurs, the intersection of politics and business trends has led to volatile results and investment trends for ideas and concepts that might otherwise have been integrated and adopted on a wider scale. For example, although Blackrock continues to exercise wide ranging influence throughout financial markets – including tokenized assets – the enthusiastic and public-facing manner that CEO Larry Fink has embraced and pursued ESG goals and targets has ruffled feathers across various subsets of the economic landscape. To that end, the 2024 U.S. election was decided – to at least some extent – by the backlash against ideas that some voters, investors, and policy advocates had received preferential treatment at the expense of other businesses, business models, and entrepreneurial actions. Dissecting the minutia of Presidential elections is beyond the scope of this text, but the same trends that are driving changes in business at large are also changing world of accounting and financial reporting.

PE and the Commodification of Accounting

The influx of PE money into the accounting profession is not necessarily a new trend or development but has recently accelerated in the post-COVID era. With even large firms such as EisnerAmper and CBIZ taking billions of PE capital during the last decade, leading to widespread changes within the firms and by extension the profession itself, the ramifications of these changes are still being felt. Namely, these investments have, among other items, accelerated the adoption and implementation of technologies such as RPA, AI, and GenAI tools (Hillebrand et al., 2023). In addition to the operational and efficiency related improvements that are possible as a result of these investments, they are also a leading force behind the conversations around margin pressure and other bottom-line affiliated items. By focusing primarily on the bottom-line, reimagining the traditional partnership structure of CPA firms, and advancing the adoption of technologies across the board, PE is one of the most important non-technological forces driving innovation in the profession.

In recent years, a growing number of mid-sized and large accounting firms have begun accepting PE investments, reshaping the traditional partnership model and signaling a transformative shift across the profession. These investments are not only changing firm structures but also driving aggressive growth strategies, expanded service offerings, and significant investments in technology and talent. Five noteworthy examples – EisnerAmper, Cherry Bekaert, Baker Tilly, Aprio, and Wipfli – highlight the various paths firms are taking as they navigate the PE frontier.

EisnerAmper was one of the first major U.S. accounting firms to embrace PE when it partnered with TowerBrook Capital Partners in 2021. To facilitate the deal while maintaining audit independence, the firm transitioned from a traditional partnership to a corporate structure. This change allowed EisnerAmper to separate its attest and non-attest functions, paving the way for external capital infusion.[1] The firm rapidly scaled its advisory and outsourced CFO services, significantly increased its investment in client-facing technology, and introduced expanded equity incentives for non-partner professionals to help attract and retain top talent.

Cherry Bekaert followed suit with an investment from Parthenon Capital in 2022. Like EisnerAmper, Cherry Bekaert adopted a corporate governance model to streamline decision making and better integrate new service lines. With PE backing, the firm aggressively expanded its geographic footprint through acquisitions and targeted growth in high-demand areas such as government contracting, digital transformation, and wealth management. The firm also brought in executive leaders from outside the CPA profession to help steer newly developed business units, reflecting a broader shift toward multidisciplinary leadership.[2]

Baker Tilly, although not yet fully committed to a PE deal as of early 2024, has been preparing for one by making key structural changes. These include the separation of attest and non-attest services and internal investments in digital automation through a newly formed venture capital arm. This initiative is focused on integrating AI and advanced analytics into tax and audit processes.[3] In tandem, the firm adjusted its partner compensation structure to include more performance-based metrics and equity-like rewards, aligning with the expectations of potential investors.

Aprio secured a significant PE investment from Charlesbank Capital Partners in 2023.[4] This infusion catalyzed a full rebranding from a traditional CPA firm into a broader advisory-led professional services organization. Post-investment, Aprio acquired more than 10 specialized firms in less than two years, adding capabilities in cybersecurity, digital forensics, and cloud services. The firm also launched a centralized onboarding and service delivery platform to enhance client experience and operational efficiency. Aprio's strategy included global expansion efforts, securing partnerships in Latin America and Europe to meet the needs of multinational clients.

Wipfli, while still in exploratory talks with PE firms as of late 2023, has already begun aligning its business with expectations typical of a PE deal.[5] The firm strategically diversified its service portfolio, building out significant capabilities in

---

[1]https://www.towerbrook.com/eisneramper-announces-investment-by-towerbrook-capital-partners/

[2]https://www.cbh.com/newsroom/cherry-bekaert-announces-strategic-investment-from-parthenon-capital/

[3]https://www.internationalaccountingbulletin.com/news/baker-tilly-alirriums/

[4]https://www.aprio.com/aprio-announces-strategic-growth-investment-from-charlesbank-capital-partners-ins-firmnews/

[5]https://www.pehub.com/eisneramper-wipfli-hope-to-attract-new-pe-investments-sources-say/

technology consulting, managed services, and healthcare advisory. Through its "Wipfli Digital" division, the firm has actively recruited tech talent such as engineers, data scientists, and AI developers, underscoring a move away from purely accounting-focused growth. Like its peers, Wipfli is also examining structural models that would allow it to separate attest and advisory functions to comply with independence regulations if a PE investment materializes.

Across these five firms, several consistent themes emerge: the transition from partnership to corporate models, acceleration of mergers and acquisitions, increased investment in digital infrastructure, and a fundamental shift in how talent is recruited and rewarded. These developments reflect a reimagining of what an accounting firm can be – less constrained by legacy structures and more aligned with the fast-paced expectations of capital markets and modern clients. As more firms consider the PE route, the accounting profession itself is being reshaped into a hybrid model that blends traditional assurance services with forward-looking advisory, digital, and data-driven capabilities.

While these changes and investments are already occurring within the accounting profession, there are also forces and changes that are driving change in both business at large as well as the profession; cost efficiencies and cost saving initiatives. One that is notable and has received large amounts of media attention – both positive and negative – are the governmental efficiency and cost slashing efforts that have gone by the acronym DOGE. With DOGE efforts and initiatives having been reduced in scope as of May 2025, the ramifications and findings of DOGE have reinvigorated efforts to increase transparency and cost efficiencies across the proverbial board.

Government Transparency Efforts

While the governmental efficiency efforts that have been spearheaded by Elon Musk, the Department of Governmental Efficiency (DOGE) have generated quite a large amount of push back and interest from both sides of the political spectrum the efforts and discoveries that have been made by Musk and his team have been substantial. Setting aside some of the more salacious headlines and comments that have been made, the accounting profession is also finding itself in the crosshairs of governmental efficiency efforts. Specifically, Deloitte has recently found itself in the crosshairs of governmental crackdown efforts, with an estimated $2–3 billion in revenue at risk of being eliminated as a result. With the sheer size of the firm, this is unlikely to result in long-lasting financial detriments to the firm itself but will be something looked at across the accounting profession. Let's take a look at some of the specifics below.

Since early 2025, Deloitte has been significantly impacted by the DOGE, an initiative launched under President Donald Trump's second term and led by Elon Musk. DOGE has aggressively targeted excessive government spending on private consulting contracts, and Deloitte has borne the brunt of these cuts. At least 127 of Deloitte's federal contracts have been terminated or modified – more than double that of any other consulting firm – with a combined value exceeding $1.16 billion. These actions have resulted in an estimated $371.8 million in taxpayer savings, including the cancelation of a $51 million IT services contract with the Department of Health and Human Services. Deloitte's Government and Public Services division, which employs over 15,000 individuals, has begun reallocating personnel from affected projects and is preparing for potential layoffs.[6] The broader consulting industry is also feeling the pressure: Booz Allen Hamilton saw 61 contracts cut totaling $207.1 million, while Accenture faced 30 terminations worth $240.2 million.[7] In response, the General Services Administration has mandated that all consultancies provide detailed justifications for their existing contracts, with a clear emphasis on cutting costs and eliminating non-essential services. These developments signal a broader shift in federal procurement strategy and present ongoing challenges for Deloitte's public sector operations.

Even as some of the existing revenue and work streams that have long powered the non-attest and non-tax growth of CPA firms continue to come under fire, the reality is that entirely new business lines and revenue opportunities are emerging on an almost daily basis. One of the most important developments and others of growth for CPA firms, and even CPA-adjacent firms, are the opportunities present as they are related to tokenized assets. Especially as tokenized assets or on-chain assets become better integrated within the TradFi sector, CPA firms are taking note. Let's take a look at how the development of tokenized assets, including their growth and greater utilization, are altering the business landscape.

Tokenized Assets

Bitcoin, crypto, and the wider tokenized asset landscape continue to dominate headlines and news coverage across financial markets. With traditional financial firms such as Fidelity and Blackrock creating and issuing products that have, in turn, attracted tens of billions of dollars in investment, the reality remains that the promise of crypto and crypto payments is slowly becoming a reality. Blockchain, on the other hand, remains an underlying technology instrument and asset that addresses multiple concerns and business cases, including payments, real estate records, title records, and healthcare information. In addition to these fast moving assets, which need to be regulated as well as monitored closely for fraud and financial malfeasance, these rapid developments also reinforce the need for continued education for policymakers, regulators, and investors alike (Chen, 2024).

---

[6]https://fortune.com/2025/04/03/doge-private-contract-crackdown-deloitte-consultancies/
https://www.businessinsider.com/deloitte-doge-consulting-crackdown-contracts-cuts-big-four-2025-4#:~:text=The%20Trump%20administration%20is%20slashing,save%20taxpayers%20about%20$371.8%20million
https://www.highergov.com/news/list-of-all-contracts-terminated-by-doge-6287413
https://www.inc.com/bruce-crumley/deloitte-layoffs-reflect-private-sector-fallout-from-doge-cuts-to-government-contracts/91171831

[7]https://www.inc.com/bruce-crumley/layoffs-hit-consulting-giant-booz-allen-as-doge-cancelled-contracts-take-a-toll/91194205

Focusing specifically on the rapid developments and changes that have occurred in the bitcoin and cryptoasset sector in 2024, there are several elements that are worth highlighting. Beginning in January 2024, the approval of spot bitcoin ETFs by the SEC – following years of denying such products and waging an antagonistic campaign against crypto entrepreneurs – unleashed a proverbial tidal wave of investment and interest. Following examples set by firms such as Fidelity and Blackrock, other asset managers and investment funds have begun to advise clients to invest certain percentages of assets under management into bitcoin and other cryptoassets (Putritama et al., 2024). Following these developments, which also led to significant price increases for bitcoin and other cryptocurrencies, TradFi banking and payment processing institutions also began to embrace blockchain, tokenized assets, and especially bitcoin.

Building on efforts that were initially launched in 2023, PayPal continued to integrate blockchain and cryptoassets into operations by allowing both individual and merchant customers to buy, sell, and hold crypto using PayPal wallets. In addition to this functionality, PayPal also allows merchant customers to move crypto holdings from the hot wallet to non-PayPal cold wallets. With over 400 million customers worldwide, including a leading position in the U.S. mobile payment market, these development cannot be understated.[8] From a policy level, it is also worth noting that the U.S. federal government has also begun to integrate blockchain technology into the critically important U.S. treasury market, with approximately $2 billion in treasuries already running on-chain.[9]

The year 2025 saw further efforts by TradFi to more fully integrate cryptoassets and blockchain information within operations, specifically with the launch of JPMD by JP Morgan Chase in partnership with Coinbase.[10] By establishing a partnership between one of the largest TradFi financial firms in the United States and one of the most well regarded crypto-native organizations in the United States is sure to have an outsized impact on the space. Specifically since the stablecoin/demand deposit hybrid has promised many of the benefits of both on-chain transactions and traditional deposit options, this project is almost guaranteed to attract significant investment and regulatory attention moving forward.

Tokenized assets at large as set to continue redefining financial markets and transactions as virtually every large financial institution/asset manager has embraced these technologies. Specifically the reality that U.S. treasuries – the largest and most liquid singular financial asset in the world – has begun to utilize tokenized to any extent, should serve as an indication as to how widespread and favorable the opinion toward these assets are. As these assets become more mainstream and widely accepted, the necessity for better and more comprehensive accounting rules will also increase in importance (Prokopenko et al., 2024). Even as volatility remains a somewhat integrated part of the tokenized asset landscape,

---

[8]https://www.paypal.com/li/webapps/mpp/country-worldwide

[9]https://finance.yahoo.com/news/tokenized-treasury-funds-pass-2b-182634618.html

[10]https://www.coindesk.com/business/2025/06/17/jpmorgan-introduces-usd-deposit-token-on-coinbase-s-base-blockchain

the integration of crypto (including bitcoin) within TradFi sectors is also potentially set to redefine how financial markets work as well as how investors assess risk and market volatility.

Last but not least, and prior to conducting a deeper dive into AI, two points are worth highlighting. First, GenAI is largely still an umbrella term that can mean several different items depending on the context, and the fact remains that more organizations are not equipped to successfully integrate AI within the accounting industry (Greenman et al., 2024). Specifically, the wide-ranging implications of AI across various business areas and industry workstreams are still being analyzed even as investment and interest accelerates. Second, despite the interest and investment in AI by virtually every organization in the world, the fact remains that the potential over excitement and investment in this sector has potentially produced a bubble-like environment in which there will likely be significant failures prior to substantial commercial successes (Bou Reslan & Jabbour Al Maalouf, 2024).

The economic and business landscape for accounting and auditing professionals is undergoing a substantial shift in multiple ways, even as the profession also faces challenges in via pipeline talent issues, non-accounting firm competition, and generally higher expectations for real-time granular financial data. Trends and forces that are driving change can be difficult to narrow down by the simultaneous rise of AI, ESG, and growing investment into tokenized assets together capture the plurality of forces and dynamics that will make the world of accounting tomorrow very different from the current landscape. No singular text can address all of these wide ranging issues, but understanding the big picture is imperative to conduct further and more in-depth analytics.

References

Bou Reslan, F., & Jabbour Al Maalouf, N. (2024). Assessing the transformative impact of AI adoption on efficiency, fraud detection, and skill dynamics in accounting practices. *Journal of Risk and Financial Management*, *17*(12), 577. https://doi.org/10.3390/jrfm17120577

Chen, K.-S. (2024). Investigating the impact of financial reporting for cryptocurrencies on company value. *Journal of Applied Finance & Banking*, *14*(3), 111–130. https://doi.org/10.47260/jafb/1436

Choi, S. U., & Lee, W. J. (2024). Financial statement comparability and environmental, social, and governance (ESG) performance. *Sustainability*, *16*(18), 7993. https://doi.org/10.3390/su16187993

Comoli, M., Tettamanzi, P., & Murgolo, M. (2023). Accounting for 'ESG' under disruptions: A systematic literature network analysis. *Sustainability*, *15*(8), 6633. https://doi.org/10.3390/su15086633

Greenman, C., Esplin, D., Johnston, R., & Richards, J. (2024). An analysis of the impact of artificial intelligence on the accounting profession. *Journal of Accounting Education and Practice*, 25(2), 188. https://doi.org/10.60154/jaepp.2024.v25n2p188

Hillebrand, L., Berger, A., Deußer, T., Dilmaghani, T., Khaled, M., Kliem, B., Loitz, R., Pielka, M., Leonhard, D., Bauckhage, C., & Sifa, R. (2023). *Improving zero-shot text matching for financial auditing with large language models*. arXiv. https://arxiv.org/abs/2308.06111

Lorne, F., & Li, T. (2024). ESG accounting – The principles and principals to be served? *Theoretical Economics Letters*, *14*, 1513–1521. https://doi.org/10.4236/tel.2024.144075

Prokopenko, O., Koldovskiy, A., Khalilova, M., Orazbayeva, A., & Machado, J. (2024). Development of blockchain technology in financial accounting. *Computation*, *12*(12), 250. https://doi.org/10.3390/computation12120250

Putritama, A., Warsono, S., Ali, S., & Handayani, W. (2024). The impact of blockchain technology on accounting: A literature review. *Complex Systems Informatics and Modeling Quarterly*, *41*, 40–54. https://doi.org/10.7250/csimq.2024-41.03

Chapter 2

Artificial Intelligence

Abstract

Artificial intelligence (AI) is transforming corporate governance; risk management; and environmental, social, and governance (ESG) reporting, driving fundamental shifts in business decision making. AI integration enhances transparency, fraud detection, and operational efficiency but raises ethical concerns, governance challenges, and disclosure requirements. Firms must develop oversight frameworks to balance AI innovation with accountability. Large language models (LLMs), such as ChatGPT, introduce both opportunities and risks related to data privacy, corporate governance, and workforce impacts. As AI adoption accelerates, accounting and financial service professionals must address job displacement, evolving fraud prevention strategies, and the need for human oversight to mitigate ethical drift and preserve trust.

Keywords: Artificial intelligence; corporate governance; ESG reporting; fraud detection; large language models; financial services employment

What is Artificial Intelligence?

AI is a field of computer science that, while it has existed for decades in various forms, has more recently experienced a surge in interest and investment following the launch of ChatGPT and other various models. Beginning with the expert systems and other rules-based intelligence matrices popularized following World War 2 the pace of development stagnated for until the physical capabilities of chips and the processing power of the computers themselves were able to keep pace with market expectations.

With the launch of ChatGPT in November 2022, the conversation around AI has rapidly evolved and developed to include a wide range of products and

Artificial Intelligence, ESG Investments and the Future of Tokenized Assets, 11–24

doi:10.1108/978-1-83708-108-020261002

services; for the context of accounting and financial services professionals, it makes sense to begin the AI conversation with details about the type of AI in discussion. We can also observe how the rise of LLMs is driving the narrative and wider conversation around AI both in the financial world and other economic areas.

Prior to discussing AI in a more comprehensive manner relating strictly to business implementation, it is useful to define the various aspects and subsets of AI that exist and that institutions are further developing. I provide a summary of these below, but the list is not comprehensive:

- *Narrow AI*: Narrow or specific AI is generally considered the most basic level of AI, which can also be associated with automation or more routine kinds such as batch posting transactions or producing automated financial reports. This subset of AI is most often categorized as the automation or routine tasks, transactions, or processes within a specific software program or organization. Importantly, this level of AI cannot be applied to different data sets of areas of the organization and is limited to the specific data sets on which it was trained.
- *General AI*: The subset of AI labeled as general AI is the class and type of AI that has been most commonly implemented at organizations across different business lines and economic areas. This type of AI is most often associated with automation, analytics, or other benefits generated via these tools and their transfer over to different data sets or areas of the organization. For example, a general or strong AI program would be able to be trained on a certain set of data, learn patterns, and generate insights (on personnel data, for example), and take those lessons and insights and apply them to other related data sets such as benefits or retirement data.
- *Cognitive computing*: The rise of ChatGPT and other chat-driven AI models has led some market commentators to speculate and forecast that the rise of cognitive computing has already arrived. While it might seem that some of the AI models in the marketplace have the ability to learn and improve over time, true cognitive computing remains both beyond the budget and scope of most organizations to successfully integrate. Despite the range of AI that exists and continues to permeate the marketplace, one kind of AI has created an intuitive and easy to use version of AI; LLMs.

AI Governance

Any conversation of analysis of AI and the implications of AI on the business environment must also discuss and mention the impact that AI will have on corporate governance, which in turn indicates that AI will, indirectly, also drive changes and new ways of thinking in the fields of ESG (Tandiono & Goel, 2023). While still an emerging technology that is being worked on and the impact of AI is still being projected and analyzed, there are several core ways and questions that have already arisen as they connect to AI and corporate governance. Let's take a look at a few of them below.

AI is poised to revolutionize corporate governance, bringing a wave of transformation that extends beyond data analytics and automation. As AI technologies become increasingly integrated into business operations, they are reshaping how companies make decisions, manage risks, and uphold transparency. The implications of AI, especially as an increasingly large amount of decisions are handled almost entirely by AI, are still being researched and analyzed, especially as these decisions impact employees and customers alike.

In the realm of decision-making, AI-driven analytics offer corporate boards unprecedented access to data-driven insight (Smith & Doe, 2024). Predictive models powered by AI can forecast market trends and identify potential risks, enabling more informed and strategic planning. This shift toward AI-enhanced decision making allows companies to navigate complex business environments with greater agility and precision.

Risk management is another area undergoing significant transformation due to AI integration. AI systems excel at detecting fraud, identifying irregularities, and ensuring compliance through real-time monitoring (Hasan, 2024). Advanced algorithms can pinpoint vulnerabilities, particularly in cybersecurity, providing a robust defense against evolving threats. This proactive approach to risk management not only safeguards company assets but also bolsters stakeholder confidence.

Transparency and accountability are being redefined in the AI era. Automated financial reporting and regulatory compliance tools reduce the margin for human error, ensuring accuracy and reliability in disclosures. The fusion of AI with blockchain technology further enhances the security and verifiability of audit trails, reinforcing corporate integrity and trustworthiness. Even as some professionals and practitioners fear being replaced by AI, it should be treated more as an advisory tool versus a potential adversary (Brown, 2023). However, the integration of AI into corporate governance is not without challenges. Ethical considerations, such as addressing biases in AI decision-making and ensuring fairness, are paramount. Corporate boards must establish comprehensive frameworks to oversee responsible AI use, balancing innovation with ethical obligations. This includes fostering AI literacy among board members and potentially reshaping board composition to include AI expertise.

Operational efficiency stands to gain immensely from AI adoption. Automation of routine tasks reduces operational costs and frees up human resources for more strategic initiatives. AI-powered tools enhance communication and information flow among board members, facilitating more cohesive and timely decision-making processes.

Strategically, AI serves as a catalyst for innovation. By uncovering new business opportunities and optimizing existing operations, AI-driven governance frameworks position companies for sustained growth and competitiveness in the market. Embracing AI not only future-proofs organizations but also equips them to adapt to the rapidly evolving digital landscape. An exciting proposition to be sure, but also one that can threaten the margins and growth potential of advisory-oriented business lines and firms.

The automation and augmentation of business decision making that will accompany AI implementation will certainly deliver benefits to the organizations in question, but there will also need to be measures taken to ensure that the automation does not supersede the authority or decision-making processes currently in place. In other words, there will consistently be a need for human oversight and review, even as automation and AI integration continues to accelerate across industry verticals.

AI Governance Disclosures

In addition to the governance issues that will continue to rise with regards to AI implementation, there are also going to be changes related to the types and quantity of information that will need to be disclosed and reported to the marketplace (Mirzaie, 2025). Even as regulators and other authoritative bodies struggle to implement and deal with the tidal waves of AI that are coming to the marketplace, there is going to be a need for firms to develop standardized frameworks and evaluative benchmarks with which to judge the quality and effectiveness of AI disclosure. These AI disclosure issues will include, but are not limited to, the following.

The impact of AI on employee training and retention. One significant issue that has continued to become mainstream news coverage and focus for upper management is that most recent entrants to the workforce are making a different use of AI versus previous generations. Specifically, the fast growing Gen-Z age cohort that is rapidly entering and expanding into the workforce is implementing AI in a unique way. Leveraging AI to apply to thousands of job applications, and ultimately ghosting or ignoring employer follow-ups, is changing how employers will need to attract and retain employees going forward. While the impacts of AI on employee hiring and retention will impact every organization, there are several points that will need to be disclosed going forward.

First, are there policies in place within the organization that will help guide and govern how AI will be used to handle and analyze sensitive data, including the personally identifiable information of customers and clients. This is going to be a concern regardless of which industry is being reported and is going to lead to the development of standardized frameworks for the disclosure of such effects.

Second, are there going to need to be changes to debt covenants and stock reporting policies given the instantaneous and rapid ability of AI-led applications to manage, adjust, and tweak the financial ratios of the company. For instance, if firms report earnings on a quarterly basis that only means that the information related to the firm are being reported four times a year, whereas AI-governed liquidity and cash flow metrics can be governed on a minute-to-minute basis. Linking back to the previous section, as AI increasingly directs and governs the organization and organizational decision-making, how will this affect the financial health and reporting policies of the firm?

Third, are the specific models of AI going to be implemented going to require disclosures and reporting related to how these models work? Specifically are the

AI tools going to need to have specific technical information disclosed about them, or are generalities going to be enough to satisfy the investing marketplace?

One other aspect of the disclosure around AI is the question as to how the data sharing relationships and connections and going to be reported and disclosed (Modisane, 2024). For instance, while many large and well-established/funded organizations are going to have the functionality to develop and build out proprietary AI tools, most firms are not going to have either the internal expertise or financial resources to do so. Given that, is the process by which the data are shared between the firm itself and AI tools – including how customer/client data are potentially shared – going to be governed via formalized processes or frameworks, or will existing cybersecurity and data policies be sufficient?

AI Impact on Fraud Detection and Prevention

One of the most impactful ways that AI can drive and innovation within the financial service space is the ability of AI to enable financial market regulators and other oversight agencies to detect, prevent, and provide redress efforts against fraud (Mgammal, 2024). According to recent market research efforts, the level of fraud and other unethical behavior seems to be increasing[1]; such a development is unacceptable with the pace of information production as well as the ever-increasing amounts of standardized and non-standardized information. Let's take a look at a few of the ways in which AI can assist firms in fraud detection, anomaly detection, and the overall reduction of fraud.

AI and Anomaly Detection

One specific way that AI is already assisting with the audit and attestation function is by allowing auditors to improve detection during the engagement planning and actual auditing process. Current auditors and audit practices do not allow the audit team to examine the entire history of transactions and interactions that have occurred during the audit period in question. Via the leveraging of AI to allow most real-time analytics and reporting of said analytics, the audit team or engagement team can instead focus on more potentially material issues. On top of being able to be more focused on material issues, this also allows the audit team, as well as regulators and enforcement agencies to be able to catch potentially unethical actions prior to them causing economic damage to various players in the marketplace. For instance, a large component of most audits and audit functions is to review transactional records for payments that are either reoccurring, to consistent in size, or that form a pattern that might raise questions. AI, with the ability to analyze virtually any information in real time on a continuous basis, will allow auditors to catch transactions that trigger red flags for the audit team. In these cases, there is a definitive benefit provided by AI, the ability to automate the

[1]https://www.ftc.gov/news-events/news/press-releases/2025/03/new-ftc-data-show-big-jump-reported-losses-fraud-125-billion-2024

journal entry, transaction, and reporting issues that need to be examined during the audit process.

Fraud Prevention

Another way in which AI can assist firms is by providing real-time insights to potentially identify unethical actions by internal actors within the organization. While better analytics will not prevent fraudulent or unethical activity, it will enable providers of financial statement data an opportunity to observe and report on gray or potentially borderline activity (Hillebrand et al., 2023). A primary example of an organization that could have been stopped before its collapse would be FTX. Clearly, the fraud and deliberate actions taken by the management team of FTX would have been able to circumvent even the most assiduous efforts of auditors and audit professionals; the reality is that by analyzing in real-time the unethical payments made by FTX to internal and external counterparties might have allowed regulators to spotlight and monitor and real-time monitoring efforts. At the very least if the market norm had transformed to one of continuous monitoring versus periodic reporting, the lack of continuous data being shown by FTX could have been viewed as a warning sign to regulators.

AI Impact on Social Capital

Another area that AI is set to impact organizations and policy alike is the area of policy and policy conversations related to employment, social equity, and the role of organizations in the evolution from shareholder to stakeholder capitalism. Whether it takes the form of universal basic income (UBI) or the potential economic displacement that could occur as AI integration continues to expand across economic lines, it will become increasingly evident that policies and economic frameworks will need to be updated as this comes to pass. Setting aside these large socio-political issues for the moment, let's take a look at a few of areas in which accounting and financial reporting will be influenced by the growing economic clout of AI.

AI-driven governance. While the pace and anticipated development of AI has seemingly outpaced the realities for the time being the fact remains that if there are corporate decisions – including capital allocation and personnel ones – being made either entirely or even partially by AI, governance metrics will need to be updated. From a financial reporting perspective, the governance rankings and scores that are used by institutional investors to rank the investability of firms will also need to be updated. Several questions that will need to be asked include, but are not limited to, the following:

- Does the integration of AI into capital allocation decisions increase or decrease the risks associated with the organization in question? These risks can include both asymmetric and symmetric risks as first adopters as well as technology laggards could experience higher-than-level volatility versus the marketplace.

- Will the decision-making process becoming more AI-driven increase or decrease the volatility of individual stocks, entire industries, or various geographic regions going forward? Notably, is there a process by which the likelihood of said changes can be assessed and standardized?
- AI-driven capital allocation also affects asset valuation and impairment assessments. Machine-learning models can improve accuracy in forecasting future cash flows, asset depreciation, and goodwill impairment, reducing the subjectivity in these estimates. However, this also raises concerns about model transparency and the need for accountants to understand and audit AI-driven financial models effectively.
- Regulatory compliance and audit processes will also need to adapt. With AI playing a larger role in decision-making, auditors must assess not only financial statements but also the algorithms and data inputs used in capital allocation. The risk of bias in AI models could introduce unintended distortions in financial reports, requiring new frameworks for AI governance.
- Additionally, AI's impact on capital allocation may lead to changes in financial statement disclosures. Investors and regulators may demand more detailed information on how AI models influence financial decisions, risk assessments, and resource allocation strategies.

Large Language Models

The iteration of AI that has garnered so much attention and focus most recently is the subset of AI known as LLMs. These applications and tools will differ depending on the parent company in question but generally tend to function along similar lines. Leveraging data sets, examples, and other information, these models are "trained" through repetitive exposure to pattern recognition, word and syntax order, and other connections that enable these models to then respond accurately to prompts (Dong et al., 2024). These examples and training models also enable the AI models to appear to be intuitive and respond in real-time to questions and prompts. These LLMs also allow the AI models to apply subject matter knowledge and expertise across different subject areas which have also helped accelerate the adoption of these models and programs by virtually every large organization across an array of economic areas.

Given the hype and excitement that has accompanied the launch and development of multiple chatbots and LLM's, it is worth reviewing how these types of AI programs are trained and developed and how they are launched into the marketplace.

First, it is imperative that financial professionals, clients, and investors understand that as powerful and interactive as many of these applications seem, these tools are still relatively simple to understand. The quality of answers given to certain questions (prompts) or the comparison and analytics performed by these tools are in direct correlation to the quality of both the prompts and the data set that the AI was trained on. In other words, this means that the AIs being used in the marketplace are still reliant on human training and data curation to be effective.

Second, and this is something that financial market professionals should remain vigilant about, is that the applicability of many open-source tools – such as ChatGPT – are going to be limited by the type, quantity, and completeness of data that is able to be shared with it. This is why many financial institutions – including those that are pursuing green or sustainability connected projects – have developed proprietary GPTs or similar programs. Such a walled-garden approach not only mimics the days of the early internet but will also limit the effectiveness of these tools over time.

Third, like any other software program or application, even the most comprehensive AI protocol will need to be updated over time, and the processes by which this occur will also need to be incorporated within the internal control structure within firms. One timely example of this need is the fact that as of January 2024, the standard answers provided by ChatGPT – the most well-known AI-augmented chatbot – were only up to date as of December 2023. Specific search queries can lead to more current results, which is yet another examples of the importance of correct prompt construction. As AI models continue to develop and accelerate rapidly, the need for a consistent and standardized approach for how said models are to be updated will also be something that needs to be reported, governed, and controlled for at organizations.

Another aspect of GPTs of all kinds or any LLM-derived chatbot is that users are going to be able to develop and deploy customized GPTs in real-time as market needs change. One example of this reality is that most firms, including the Big 4 accounting firms as well as financial services firms such as Bloomberg, have developed proprietary models to be used by employees that are based – but not dependent on – ChatGPT itself.

ChatGPT

ChatGPT is just one of the many LLMs that have entered into the marketplace since 2022 but is by far the most popular one that has entered the mass market and is the one primarily used by financial services organizations. Although earlier models and iterations of ChatGPT had relatively limited use cases and applications, and still is not universally correct or complete, the more recent and updated versions that have come to market have improved virtually across the board. It is also worth noting that the ownership structure and corporate control of OpenAI – the parent company of ChatGPT – also make the firm itself and its product a unique case study.

A Quick Review of OpenAI

OpenAI is a research and deployment company focused on developing artificial general intelligence (AGI) that benefits all of humanity. Co-founded by Sam Altman, the corporate structure that was selected is also in alignment with the belief that AGI can (and will) be of benefit to all of humanity. The firm operates under a unique corporate structure designed to align its financial incentives with its mission. Initially founded in 2015 as a nonprofit organization, OpenAI transitioned in 2019 to a "capped-profit" model under the entity OpenAI LP, a limited partnership. This structure allows it to attract investments while ensuring that profits are capped, and any surplus is reinvested toward its mission. While some comments and speculation have launched about the possibility of this corporate structure changing, as of this writing the unique hybrid structure is still intact.

The structure comprises two primary entities: OpenAI LP and OpenAI Nonprofit, which retains oversight of the company's operations and adherence to its mission. OpenAI Nonprofit appoints the board of directors for OpenAI LP and holds a majority of its voting power. This governance model ensures that OpenAI prioritizes ethical considerations and safety in the development and deployment of its AI technologies. OpenAI LP is governed by a hybrid model, combining private-sector agility with nonprofit values. It includes "capped-profit investors" who receive limited returns on their investments, after which any additional profits are directed toward OpenAI's mission. Key stakeholders include researchers, engineers, and strategic investors who align with its goals.

With the rapid success and growth of ChatGPT, however, there have also been concerns raised about how this application operates, how it will be improved and expanded upon, and ultimately where ChatGPT will fit into a rapidly evolving AI marketplace. Specifically from a financial services perspective, it is worth noting that several unique factors need to be taken into account to ensure that LLMs – including ChatGPT – continue to evolve in a manner that is both useful to users but is also cognizant of the risks involved if biases. In addition to the impact of ChatGPT specifically, it is also important to acknowledge the implications of GPT-like applications that are coming to the mass market.

DeepSeek

In January 2025, the Chinese AI app and search bot DeepSeek sent shockwaves through the technology and business landscape with the unveiling of its most advanced model to date, which was stated to be nearly as accurate as ChatGPT and other American AI models while only costing a small percentage of what U.S. models cost.

The ripple effects that reverberated through U.S. markets, the intelligence community, and the AI sector at large were immediate and significant. While the initial launch of the DeepSeek model that caused the shockwaves in markets and media occurred over a weekend, the first trading day following the launch of model created significant responses across the political and economic landscape. The Trump administration took to the airwaves, expressing caution over U.S. firms and personnel using DeepSeek, a product developed in mainland China, while also reflecting that this launch should be thought of as a Sputnik moment versus an existential threat the viability of the still-growing U.S. AI industry.

U.S. AI leaders and technology firms also took swift action to (1) analyze the product itself, (2) investigate claims related to the cost and performance of DeepSeek, and (3) cooperate with U.S. intelligence agencies as work began at unpacking just how such a product could have come to market with such little fanfare or advance warning. Specifically, several areas and points seemed to form the center of research and analysis around both DeepSeek and the potential applications of said technology. These include, but are not limited to, the following:

- *Data privacy and security*: DeepSeek's data collection practices have raised alarms about user privacy and potential misuse. The app stores substantial amounts of user data on servers located in China, which, under Chinese cybersecurity laws, can be accessed by the government upon request. This poses a risk that sensitive information could be exploited for surveillance or other purposes.
- *Intellectual property concerns*: There are allegations that DeepSeek may have utilized proprietary AI models from U.S. companies without authorization. OpenAI, for instance, is investigating claims that DeepSeek employed a technique known as "distillation" to enhance its AI model by learning from OpenAI's larger systems, potentially violating intellectual property rights.
- *National security implications*: The rapid adoption of DeepSeek within the USA has prompted national security evaluations. The White House is assessing the potential risks associated with the app, considering the possibility that it could be used for foreign influence operations, disinformation campaigns, or espionage activities.
- *Military restrictions*: In response to these concerns, the U.S. Navy has prohibited its personnel from using DeepSeek, citing potential security and ethical issues. This move underscores the apprehension within military circles about the app's origins and data handling practices.

These concerns, coupled with the announcement from Alibaba (also in January 2025) that it had also launched an AI tool on par with DeepSeek, have spurred multiple conversations and debates within the business, intelligence, and political communities. Such conversations have centered around the applications of AI for business use cases, the military applications of equivalent technologies, and the data privacy effects that ever more sophisticated AI will have on both individuals and institutions. One of the most important aspects of AI and AI adoption pertains almost directly to finance and financial services; how to combat bias and other ethical considerations as AI adoption accelerates.

AI Bias and Mitigation

One of the key elements that must be taken into account, especially in financial services but also as adoption of AI continues to extend into other economic areas, is that the biases that might be present in the minds of developers and coders must be offset and mitigated against as the AI tools become more complex. While it is safe to assume that these LLMs, as well as other AI-based and derived tools, are not purpose built with any sort of biases present, it would be illogical to conclude that no biases whatsoever are embedded within these applications. This also circles back to the importance of including ethical training and awareness within the development and testing process of both the algorithms driving AI platforms and the testing and refinement processes that drive AI from concept to market ready status.

Diving deeper into possibility of AI biases, it is worth discussing what an unconscious bias is and how it can manifest itself since, as previously noted, the large corporations (with profit motive) are extremely unlikely to develop biased programs and release them to the marketplace. For the purposes of this text, an unconscious bias can be defined as the automatic assumptions that can be made about groups of people, certain geographic or socio-economic areas, or gender roles. These biases can manifest themselves in how certain traits and pieces of information are evaluated, how different combinations of data are ranked, and ultimately how the results of analyses are used to make decisions about candidates, applications, or other job/hiring focused decisions.

Mitigating biases, especially unconscious ones, requires a conscious effort focusing on integrating diversity of thought, testing, and application throughout the development, testing, and re-testing process of said algorithms. Specific steps that can be taken, and that focus on both the employee and AI program, include but are not limited to:

1. Employee education and training around unconscious biases. As with any technologically oriented system or process improvement project, employee training and awareness are of paramount importance. This importance of training and explanatory measures only increase when automation and AI are brought into the conversation. For example, and especially for financial services (more on that later) making decisions based purely on either quantitative or qualitative factors is unacceptable; a blended approach is almost always required, but how can an AI algorithm or program be trained to do so consistently?
2. Standardized and double-blind decision-making processes. Building on that first point, the standardization of decision making is an imperative as it connects to the successful implementation of AI. A simple, yet humorous exercise that can be used to illustrate how difficult this can be is to ask employees the following question; how many steps are required to prepare a Turkey and Swiss cheese sandwich (or whatever your favorite sandwich is)? The answer will differ on the audience but is always higher, and is more complicated, than initially estimated
3. Transparency and iterative feedback. An essential part of any AI implementation process is the way in which the training and tools themselves are revised and edited over time, especially as the market continues to change and the specific use cases for firms evolve over time. Notably, one aspect that is important to keep in mind is that as employees are upskilled and the organization itself receives many of the benefits of AI that the mindset and approach to further AI implementation will – by default – evolve as well.

Adoption of AI in Accounting and Financial Services

One of the more obvious questions and concerns that have arisen over the last few years in the face of rapid AI adoption and implementation is what the impact will be on the accounting and financial service sectors. Clearly, the rise of GenAI has allowed researchers and analysts to automate and streamline large amounts of the financial reporting, analysis, and interpretation processes that historically have occupied large amounts of professional time. Building on this point, there are several other workforce and workplace effects that, while perhaps less obvious, will arguably have more significant longer term effects on the workforce at large.

Pipeline and retention issue are one of the most significant conversation topics that have become part of the mainstream conversation and are the dual issues facing accounting and financial professionals while contending with and dealing with pipeline. In short, the pipeline is the analysis of how many individuals are entering the profession versus the number of people currently working, as well as the number of people exiting the profession either via retirement or leaving the field for other reasons. AI has the potential to improve this landscape in the long-term, although it will be a volatile pathway forward. This is because the effects of AI – automating analysis and the ability to create presentations and other client facing work – will reduce the need for the number of professionals at each end of employee hierarchy. For example if crunching numbers, performing analytics, and reporting out analytics to internal and external colleagues can be automated, this means that entry level staffers and early career professionals will have less active work to do. Conversely, at the partner level of a firm, how many partners will be able to bring in the necessary levels of business (usually in the millions of dollars) with so much work that was usually performed by individuals being performed by robotics and automation.

Ultimately what is going to occur when AI becomes increasingly mainstream is that both the data creation and analytics that are performed at organizations will become more directly impacted by the nuances and tweaks that will invariably need to be performed on AI tools over time. This also highlights an important governance issue to remember – amoral drift – which, while not entirely mitigated in traditional corporate governance settings, does at least have an established list of tools and frameworks.

Amoral Drift

Something that also impacts the accounting and financial reporting process as it pertains to AI integration within organizations is the possibility of amoral drift becoming amplified. For the purpose of this text, amoral drift can be summarized as referring to the gradual erosion of ethical standards and moral considerations in decision making, often due to repeated exposure to ethically ambiguous or questionable behavior. This phenomenon can occur in individuals, organizations, or societies when moral compromises become normalized over time. Amoral drift is particularly concerning in professional and institutional settings, where small ethical lapses, if unchecked, can escalate into systemic corruption or misconduct. Factors contributing to amoral drift include organizational culture, external pressures, rationalization of unethical actions, and desensitization to moral concerns. Recognizing and addressing amoral drift requires proactive ethical training, accountability measures, and fostering a culture of integrity.

AI Impact on Accounting and Financial Services Employment

One of the core fears and perspectives that financial services professionals will need to contend with as AI integration and implementation become more mainstream is what potential paradoxical effect this will have on the job market for said professionals. On the one hand, there are expectations that as the job market accelerates adoption of AI that efficiencies will advance, improve, and ultimately create opportunities for the organizations investing heavily into AI. On the other hand, the very real risk of job displacement and dislocations that will result from AI implementation is something that will need to be addressed. Setting aside the human effect of said changes and efficiency, there is also the business effect that said improvements will create there is also the business effect that will need to be acknowledged.

First, if clients and customers are already using AI for internal purposes, and are bringing these AI documents to the meeting with accounting and financial professionals, both sides of the table will need to understand and be educated as to where/when it is appropriate to use AI and where human oversight and supervision are still required. Specifically, as it pertains to client data or proprietary data, this is essential since clients might OK with leveraging AI for internal purposes, the utilization of AI by an external advisory.

The adoption of AI by financial firms is poised to significantly reduce headcount, primarily by automating routine and repetitive tasks traditionally performed by human workers. Functions such as data entry, transaction processing, regulatory reporting, and even basic customer service are increasingly handled by AI-powered systems, which operate more efficiently and with fewer errors. In investment banking and asset management, AI-driven algorithms can analyze vast datasets faster than human analysts, allowing firms to make more informed decisions with fewer personnel.

Additionally, AI systems are improving in natural language processing and predictive analytics, enabling them to support more complex tasks like financial forecasting, fraud detection, and compliance monitoring. These advances reduce the need for large teams of analysts and compliance officers. Moreover, firms are leveraging AI-powered chatbots and virtual assistants to handle customer inquiries, minimizing the demand for call center staff.

While AI adoption creates new roles in areas like data science and AI governance, these tend to require specialized skills and are far fewer in number than the jobs displaced. As a result, financial firms can achieve significant cost savings and operational efficiency through AI, often with a leaner workforce – leading to concerns about long-term employment prospects within the sector.

In either case and no matter how AI is adopted over time, the fact remains that the effect on employment might be negative going forward. This is why it is so important, both within the accounting and financial services industry as well as in other economic sectors, that education, training, and upskilling remain paramount. Such focus must also extend to other emerging areas of financial reporting and disclosure – ESG reporting and other issues.

References

Brown, R. (2023). Should accountants be afraid of AI? Risks and opportunities of artificial intelligence in accounting. *Accounting Horizons*. https://doi.org/10.2308/HORIZONS-2023-042

Dong, M. M., Stratopoulos, T. C., & Wang, V. X. (2024). *A scoping review of ChatGPT research in accounting and finance*. arXiv. https://arxiv.org/abs/2412.05731

Hasan, L. (2024). The role of artificial intelligence in eliminating accounting errors. *Journal of Risk & Financial Management*, *17*(8), 353.

Hillebrand, L., Berger, A., Deußer, T., Dilmaghani, T., Khaled, M., Kliem, B., Loitz, R., Pielka, M., Leonhard, D., Bauckhage, C., & Sifa, R. (2023). *Improving zero-shot text matching for financial auditing with large language models*. arXiv. https://arxiv.org/abs/2308.06111

Mirzaie, F. (2025). The impact of artificial intelligence on accounting. *AI Tech in Behavioral and Social Sciences*, *3*(1), 124–136. https://doi.org/10.61838/kman.aitech.3.1.12

Mgammal, M. H. (2024). The influence of artificial intelligence as a tool for future economies on accounting procedures: Empirical evidence from Saudi Arabia. *Discover Computing*, *27*, 20. https://doi.org/10.1007/s10791-024-09452-7

Modisane, C. (2024). *Artificial intelligence driven accounting: Benefits, risks, and the future*. ICAETM 2024 Conference Proceedings.

Smith, J., & Doe, A. (2024). Exploring accounting and AI using topic modelling. *Journal of Accounting Information*, 100709. https://doi.org/10.1016/j.accinf.2024.100709

Tandiono, S., & Goel, M. (2023). The impact of artificial intelligence on accounting. *AI Tech in Behavioral and Social Sciences*, *3*(1), Article 12. https://doi.org/10.61838/kman.aitech.3.1.12

Chapter 3

Environmental, Social, and Governance Reporting

Abstract

Environmental, social, and governance (ESG) reporting continues to reshape accounting and financial reporting by expanding the scope of disclosures beyond traditional financial statements. Rooted in historical environmental legislation, ESG reporting now encompasses both quantitative and qualitative data, influencing decision making and investor expectations. The multiple capital model (MCM) helps quantify diverse forms of value – financial, manufactured, intellectual, human, social, and natural capital – supporting integrated reporting practices. This evolution aligns with the broader shift toward stakeholder capitalism, emphasizing corporate responsibility for externalities affecting communities and ecosystems. Despite political headwinds, ESG reporting remains integral to modern corporate governance and transparency.

Keywords: ESG reporting; multiple capital model; integrated reporting; stakeholder capitalism; externalities; corporate governance

Introduction

Another megatrend that continues to reshape the accounting and financial reporting landscape is the continued evolution and development of ESG reporting. One of the core tenants of this reporting paradigm is that in order to present a full and accurate picture of how an organization is performing, it is necessary to expand reporting beyond the traditional financial statements as well as including both quantitative and qualitative information (Lorne & Li, 2024). As noted above, this reporting framework and mindset has unfortunately been in more recent times associated closely with political discourse, which has hampered further adoption

Artificial Intelligence, ESG Investments and the Future of Tokenized Assets, 25–33

doi:10.1108/978-1-83708-108-020261003

and improvement of reporting standards post 2020. Even with this discourse and the headwinds that have accelerated in the post-2020 era, the reality is that the gathering and reporting of broader ranges of information are simultaneously (1) increasing in popularity and (2) increasingly expected by reporting authorities and governments and (3) do play a role in how organizations perform overall. In other words, ESG reporting is here to stay, so it is well worth the time of any financial professional to understand how this reporting framework evolved, pros and cons that have been linked to it, and how this mindset continues to influence financial decision making.

Background of ESG

In brief, the background and history of ESG reporting is much longer than some investors and policy wonks might otherwise expect. Following the Clean Air & Water Act and the establishment of Environmental Protection Agency, the message sent to businesses by policymakers was clear; environmental and environmental-adjacent issues were to be prioritized alongside traditional financial reporting measures. Although these reporting mandates have almost universally faced opposition and pushback from industry actors, with specifics depending on the industry in question, several financially oriented tactics and strategies emerged to assist corporate America in adapting to these new requirements and expectations.

Multiple Capital Model

An interesting approach that sought to quantify and standardize reporting around some of the more qualitative areas of data that were to be collected and reported was the creation of the MCM. In essence, the concept behind the MCM was to allow organizations and financial professionals employed therein to quantify and report different forms of capital and information in a manner similar to what is already assembled and reported on a financial basis, which has carried through to ESG reporting in the post-COVID era (Christensen et al., 2024). Specifically, this mindset resulted in the creation of manufactured capital, natural capital, social and relational capital, human capital, intellectual capital, and financial capital. Working definitions for these types of capital are provided below:

- *Financial capital*: The pool of funds, including debt, equity, and retained earnings, that organizations use to finance operations and generate future value for stakeholders.
- *Manufactured capital*: Physical assets like buildings, machinery, and infrastructure that are used to produce goods or services and contribute to organizational value creation.
- *Intellectual capital*: Knowledge-based assets, including patents, brands, processes, and systems, that enhance innovation, efficiency, and differentiation in the organization's value proposition.

- *Human capital*: The skills, experience, and capabilities of employees, along with their motivation, well-being, and alignment with the organization's mission and objectives.
- *Social and relationship capital*: The relationships and networks with stakeholders, including trust, shared norms, and collaboration, that support operational stability and social license to operate.
- *Natural capital*: The environmental resources, such as air, water, and biodiversity, that organizations depend on for inputs and impact through their operations.

Integrated Reporting

Integrated reporting can be best thought of as an extension of the MCM in terms of how data are collected and reported to the marketplace, with a focus on non-financial information as well as non-standardized data.

In contemporary business environments, stakeholders expect more than mere financial profitability: they seek comprehensive insights into how organizations generate value and how their activities impact society and the environment. Integrated reporting (hereafter, "IR") has emerged as a response to this desire. It seeks to summarize, within a cohesive framework, how financial results relate to broader risks, governance mechanisms, and long-term strategy.

Definition and Conceptual Framework

Integrated reporting, as formalized by the International Integrated Reporting Council (IIRC) and consolidated under the IFRS Foundation, presents a principles-based framework that articulates how value creation occurs over multiple time horizons. It focuses on six types of "capitals."

An IR communicates how an organization's strategy, governance, performance, and prospects are interwoven with its stewardship of, and reliance upon, these capitals. Unlike traditional reporting, which is often fragmented into financial statements and disaggregated ESG disclosures, IR seeks to integrate these elements into a coherent narrative.

The Relationship Between IR and Accounting Practice

Accounting and finance professionals play a central role in the effective implementation of IR. Whereas conventional accounting focuses on historical financial results – recorded via income statements, balance sheets, and cash flow statements – IR requires a more expansive approach. Accountants are now expected to:

- *Measure and value non-financial resources*: Quantifying ESG metrics (such as carbon emissions, resource efficiency, and social impact) and valuing intangible assets (e.g., intellectual property, brand equity, and human capital) demands methodologies that align rigorously with accounting principles.

- *Conduct materiality assessments*: Traditional frameworks emphasize financial materiality; IR mandates the inclusion of broader strategic and sustainability-related concerns. Accountants are required to develop multi-dimensional materiality frameworks that balance quantitative data with qualitative insights.
- *Provide assurance on ESG disclosures*: Given the growing investor reliance on non-financial data, IR places elevated importance on assurance. Accountants are increasingly expected to design internal controls and seek third-party verification to uphold credibility and comparability.
- *Engage in strategic decision-making*: With IR, accountants shift from historical reporting to forward-looking roles. They participate in scenario planning, risk management, and integrated thinking – evaluating, for example, how climate risk may influence long-term capital expenditures.

The Role of Finance Function and Capital Allocation

From the perspective of financial management, IR provides a structured approach to assess long-term value creation that transcends financial returns. Through integration, finance professionals can:

- Align budgeting, forecasting, and capital expenditure processes with sustainable objectives – such as emissions reduction or workforce development – thus reconciling financial and sustainability goals.
- Incorporate ESG considerations into enterprise risk management frameworks and financial models, enhancing the robustness of scenario analysis.
- Evaluate investments by considering risk-adjusted returns as well as social and environmental impact, thereby aligning capital deployment with stakeholder expectations.
- Strengthen stakeholder communication by producing disclosures that coherently align financial results with ESG data, thereby improving trust and transparency among investors, regulators, and other stakeholders.

This paradigm also catalyzes cross-functional collaboration: finance and sustainability functions converge to construct integrated reports, embedding non-financial considerations within financial planning and analysis.

Challenges and Limitations

Despite its conceptual appeal, the adoption of IR encounters several obstacles:

1. *Standardization*: Although frameworks such as Sustainability Accounting Standards Board (SASB), Global Reporting Initiative (GRI), and Task Force on Climate-related Financial Disclosures (TCFD) provide guidance, a universally accepted standard for integrating financial and non-financial data remains nascent.

2. *Data integrity and systems*: Reliable collection, measurement, and verification of ESG data demand investment in IT systems, data governance, and process frameworks comparable to those for financial information.
3. *Cultural transformation*: Achieving integrated thinking requires organizational change. Boards and executives must reconceptualize performance measurement and broaden their definitions of success beyond financial metrics.
4. *Assurance complexity*: The assurance process for non-financial metrics presents emerging challenges, including establishing measurement standards and ensuring independence of third-party verifiers.

Integrated reporting has gained traction in certain regions, with regulatory developments such as the European Union's Corporate Sustainability Reporting Directive (CSRD) reinforcing its importance. In the USA, despite slower regulatory uptake, major corporations – such as Microsoft, Coca-Cola, and Salesforce – have begun adopting IR elements in their annual and sustainability reporting, signaling its growing relevance as a tool for transparency and stakeholder engagement.

In sum, integrated reporting offers a transformative model for how organizations communicate value creation. It encourages a unified view of financial performance, strategy, risk management, and sustainability. For accounting and finance professionals, IR represents both a challenge and an opportunity: a challenge to master non-financial domains and design robust assurance frameworks, and an opportunity to occupy a more strategic role in guiding organizations toward sustainable long-term value creation. As markets increasingly prioritize resilience, purpose, and transparency, IR is poised to become not merely a best practice, but a necessary standard for credible corporate reporting.

Stakeholder Capitalism

The rise of ESG reporting, including the development of the MCM during that process, is also indicative of a broader shift in the financial reporting landscape; the pivot away from purely focusing on shareholder value creation and returns to a broader definition of growth in the form of stakeholder capitalism. At the core of the idea, stakeholder capitalism is the mindset and reporting approach that dictates firms should, of course, focus on generating financial returns for investors and stakeholders, but in addition to this focus, that firms should also focus on the benefits that are able to be created and derive from providing value to the wider community within which the firm operates (Comoli et al., 2023). Arising in almost direct response to the 1970s and 1980s explicit focus on the proverbial bottom line, the advent of stakeholder capitalism has at its core several components that need to be focused on for the concept to be fully understood.

In today's interconnected and socially conscious business environment, the concept of stakeholder reporting has grown significantly in relevance. While traditional accounting practices primarily focused on financial performance for shareholders, stakeholder reporting expands the focus to include a broader range of interested parties – employees, customers, regulators, communities, suppliers, and civil society. As businesses are increasingly held accountable for their ESG impacts, stakeholder reporting and accounting practices are evolving to provide a more holistic view of organizational performance and responsibility.

In the past, companies mostly talked about performance in terms of profits, share price, and financial health – information aimed squarely at shareholders. But the world has changed. Today's businesses are expected to be accountable to a much broader audience: employees, customers, suppliers, regulators, communities, and the environment itself. That's where stakeholder reporting comes in.

Stakeholder reporting is about more than just financial results. It's about providing clear, credible insight into how a company operates, how it affects the world around it, and how it plans to create long-term value – not just for shareholders, but for everyone who has a stake in the business. It focuses on topics like environmental performance, diversity and inclusion, labor practices, ethical sourcing, and corporate governance. This broader view is increasingly seen as essential – not just by watchdogs and activists, but by investors, customers, and even employees.

Organizations now rely on frameworks like the GRI, the SASB, and the TCFD to help structure and guide their stakeholder reporting. These standards push companies to look beyond the bottom line, asking: What is our carbon footprint? How are we treating our people? Are we acting with integrity? And are we doing what we say we're doing?

Why Accountants Matter in Stakeholder Reporting

You might think that stakeholder reporting is a job for sustainability teams or public relations departments – but accountants and finance professionals are more involved than ever. In fact, they're essential to making stakeholder reporting work.

Why? Because stakeholder reports rely on data – lots of it – and accountants are the people best equipped to gather, validate, and communicate that data. Just as financial reporting depends on careful measurement and control, stakeholder reporting depends on the same precision and accountability.

Here are five ways accounting professionals are playing a central role:

- *Building the data foundation*: Stakeholder reporting depends on reliable information from all corners of the business. Accountants are often tasked with integrating ESG metrics into enterprise systems – ensuring the data are accurate, timely, and auditable. Whether it's tracking emissions, water use, or employee turnover, the data need structure and controls, much like a general ledger.
- *Helping decide what matters*: Not every issue carries the same weight. Accountants are trained to assess risk and materiality – skills that are now being

applied beyond finances. They help companies decide which stakeholder issues are truly critical, combining data analysis with stakeholder input to identify what should be disclosed.

- *Creating assurance and confidence*: As companies publish more non-financial data, stakeholders want to know they can trust it. That's where assurance comes in. Accountants help design internal checks and balances, and many firms also conduct third-party assurance reviews to verify ESG claims. The more reliable the data, the more meaningful the story.
- *Linking strategy and performance*: Today's finance teams are increasingly involved in setting and tracking key performance indicators that tie financial and non-financial goals together. For example, tracking greenhouse gas emissions per dollar of revenue, or linking executive pay to employee engagement scores. These metrics reflect how well a company is delivering value – not just to investors, but to society.
- *Navigating complex rules and regulations*: Regulatory expectations are evolving rapidly. In Europe, the CSRD is raising the bar for sustainability disclosures. In the USA, the SEC is pushing for more climate-related disclosures. Accountants are key players in understanding and implementing these rules – ensuring companies stay compliant and avoid reputational risk.

Why It Matters: The Strategic Value of Stakeholder Reporting

Stakeholder reporting isn't just about looking good – it's about making better decisions and earning trust in the process. A well-structured stakeholder report can help companies:

- Spot risks earlier
- Make smarter investments
- Improve employee morale and retention
- Strengthen customer loyalty
- Attract purpose-driven investors

That's because ESG data often highlight trends that financial statements alone can't reveal. For instance, rising absenteeism may signal a workplace culture issue. Or a heavy reliance on carbon-intensive suppliers might pose a long-term risk if climate regulations tighten. When companies view these data alongside financial performance, they can uncover new insights – and new opportunities.

And there's a reputational side to all of this too. Today's stakeholders expect companies to be transparent about their challenges as well as their successes. The organizations that are honest, consistent, and data-driven in their stakeholder communications tend to earn more trust – and often outperform in the long run.

The Challenges Ahead

Of course, stakeholder reporting isn't easy. Many companies face real challenges in getting it right:

- Standardization is tricky. ESG metrics are still evolving, and comparing one company to another isn't always straightforward.
- Assurance is still developing. Unlike financial audits, ESG assurance practices vary widely.
- Resources are limited. Especially for small- to mid-sized companies, collecting and verifying non-financial data can be a heavy lift.
- Culture matters. For stakeholder reporting to be meaningful, it has to be more than a checkbox. It requires leadership buy-in and a real commitment to transparency.

But momentum is growing. From regulators to rating agencies to the public, the call for credible stakeholder reporting is getting louder. Companies that invest early – and bring their accounting teams into the process – will be better prepared for the road ahead.

Stakeholder reporting is reshaping how businesses communicate value. It's no longer enough to talk about profits alone; organizations must show how they serve people, planet, and purpose. Accounting professionals are uniquely positioned to make that happen – by ensuring the information is accurate, meaningful, and connected to long-term strategy. As expectations around corporate responsibility continue to rise, stakeholder reporting will be more than a trend. It will be a core part of how businesses earn trust, make decisions, and build a sustainable future.

Externalities. At the core of the concept of externalities lies the fact that every action and every inaction undertaken by an organization impact individuals and institutions outside of the near networks that most often come to mind. A specific example of the externality idea is that which eventually transformed into the E in ESG; the environmental effect of certain organizations on the local and regional ecosystems within which they operated. Positive externalities are assuredly possible as well, such as when hospitals and health networks open up in the certain area and provide much needed services to the community, but negative externalities do also exist (Cao & Yuan, 2024). Unfortunately, these negative externalities are both much more common and being much better understood by investors. Be it taking the form of Superfund sites or other environmentally oriented efforts to undue past pollution, the reality is the same; negative externalities and effects must be factored into the assessment of investing opportunities.

Conclusion

Stakeholder reporting represents a significant evolution in corporate disclosure, extending the scope of accountability beyond shareholders to encompass a diverse array of internal and external stakeholders. As societal, regulatory, and market expectations continue to shift toward greater transparency and sustainability, organizations are increasingly called upon to report not only financial outcomes but also their social and environmental impacts. In this context, accounting professionals play a critical role in operationalizing stakeholder reporting through their expertise in data management, risk assessment, materiality analysis, and assurance processes.

By embedding ESG considerations into traditional accounting systems and strategic decision-making frameworks, finance and accounting functions contribute meaningfully to the credibility and effectiveness of stakeholder communication. Although challenges such as data standardization, assurance quality, and organizational readiness remain, the integration of stakeholder reporting into mainstream corporate practices is accelerating. Ultimately, stakeholder reporting – supported by robust accounting practices – offers a pathway for organizations to build trust, demonstrate long-term value creation, and align corporate objectives with the broader goals of sustainable development and responsible governance.

References

Cao, J., & Yuan, S. (2024). The effects of mandatory ESG disclosure around the world. *Contemporary Accounting Research*. https://doi.org/10.1111/1475-679X.12548

Christensen, H. B., Lee, E., Maffett, M. G., & Risius, A. (2024). ESG assurance in the United States. *Review of Accounting Studies*. https://doi.org/10.1007/s11142-024-09856-2

Comoli, M., Tettamanzi, P., & Murgolo, M. (2023). Accounting for 'ESG' under disruptions: A systematic literature network analysis. *Sustainability*, *15*(8), 6633. https://doi.org/10.3390/su15086633

Lorne, F., & Li, T. (2024). ESG accounting – The principles and principals to be served? *Theoretical Economics Letters*, *14*, 1513–1521. https://doi.org/10.4236/tel.2024.144075

Chapter 4

Tokenized Assets

Abstract

This chapter explores the rapidly changing world of tokenized assets, focusing especially on bitcoin and stablecoins, and how they're becoming a larger part of global financial systems. It traces crypto's journey – from its early beginnings among libertarian and cypherpunk communities to widespread adoption by investors, institutions, and even governments. Along the way, it looks at major turning points like the launch of U.S. spot bitcoin ETFs, the fallout from the FTX scandal, and the rise of staking and stablecoin-driven business models. It also unpacks some of the big challenges still facing the space: gaps in internal controls, uneven regulations across countries, and a tendency to focus too much on the technology and not enough on real-world applications. The growing dominance of certain firms and the push by governments to issue central bank digital currencies (CBDCs) are raising new questions about privacy, surveillance, and global monetary power. Throughout, the chapter highlights how crypto's integration with mainstream finance – and its connection to broader trends like artificial intelligence and intellectual property – is creating both exciting opportunities and real risks. As crypto continues to mature, one message becomes clear: stronger audit, reporting, and accounting practices are not just helpful – they're essential.

Keywords: Bitcoin; stablecoins; crypto governance and compliance; Central bank digital currencies; audit and accounting standards

Tokenized assets, notably bitcoin, have revolutionized the financial landscape, continue to evolve and adapt as mass market adoption continues to accelerate, and even nation-states embrace campaigns to either purchase cryptoassets directly or support the idea via tokenizing fiat currencies (Goble, 2025). To that end it seems to make sense to establish context and background to the crypto sector prior to conducting a deeper dive of the asset class itself.

Artificial Intelligence, ESG Investments and the Future of Tokenized Assets, 35–44

Published under exclusive licence by Emerald Publishing Limited
doi:10.1108/978-1-83708-108-020261004

Initially posted on GitHub the original code and coding language for the bitcoin blockchain soon caught the collective eyes of the online, libertarian, and cypherpunk community. Following the minting and creation of the Genesis blockchain in January 2009 the initial adoption of bitcoin and blockchain technology proceeded at a relatively sluggish pace. Prices remained at low levels, reaching highs that remained well below $1,000 for years before – in 2017 – bitcoin burst into the mainstream financial conversation. Touching new all-time-highs of $20,000 (albeit briefly) in December 2017, the bitcoin era had officially come to both Wall Street and Main Street. Following this spectacular run-up in prices, and as often follows dramatic increases in price, the price of bitcoin and the overall cryptoasset marketplace fell into the doldrums during 2018-2019, with prices well below previous all-time-highs and only occasionally cracking the $10,000 level, only half highs previously reached.[1]

The COVID-19 global pandemic changed virtually every industry, and the cryptoasset space was not immune to these far ranging changes and effects. While the primary drivers of the price recovery and acceleration that occurred both for bitcoin and the wider cryptoasset space are numerous, there are a few that seem worthy of further examination. First during the crypto winter/doldrums of 2018–2019, there continued to be significant efforts and developments in the blockchain and cryptoasset sector. Many of the Layer 2 applications – smart contracts, stablecoins, zero-knowledge proofs, non-fungible tokens, decentralized finance, and decentralized autonomous organizations – that are driving adoption and investment in 2024 and beyond were initially developed and de-bugged during this era. Additionally, the loosening of financial conditions, including economic stimulus payments and relief in the USA and across the globe, helped encourage investors across the board to allocate funds to higher risk and higher volatility assets.[2]

Even the collapse and spectacular fraud that was uncovered at FTX, which also got its start and experienced high growth during this COVID/post-COVID era was not able to do much to mute the growth and price velocity of cryptoassets. Obviously following the collapse and subsequent trial of FTX and CEO Bankman-Fried, the price of bitcoin decreased dramatically and doubts resurfaced as to the economic viability of these assets outside of vehicles for speculation (International Monetary Fund, 2025). This all changed in 2024, however, as the first bitcoin spot ETFs were approved by the SEC for trading and purchase by U.S. investors in January. This approval kickstarted another bull market in bitcoin and other cryptoassets, led this time by institutional purchases by firms such as Blackrock and Fidelity versus the retail driven rallies that had characterized past rallies. Even as bitcoin prices remain near or above $100,000 in 2025 there

---

[1]https://www.binance.com/en/square/post/19732435184937#:~:text=A%20brief%20look%20at%20the,9%2C%202009

[2]https://www.worldbank.org/en/publication/wdr2022/brief/chapter-1-introduction-the-economic-impacts-of-the-covid-19-crisis#:~:text=The%20crisis%20had%20a%20dramatic,for%20small%20and%20microenterprises%2C%20respectively

are still lessons and reflections that should be remember as the shadow of FTX slowly recedes from mainstream financial market conversation.[3]

Lessons from FTX

The aftermath of FTX continues to send ripple effects throughout the crypto marketplace and the wider cryptoasset ecosystem. As the fraud and wrongdoing was discovered at FTX, both during the bankruptcy and during the criminal trial of Samuel Bankman-Fried, it became clear that the issues that occurred during these trials were not one-off items or issues, but rather were systemic to how the firm operated. Some of the most critical lessons that can and should be learned from the failure of FTX include but are not limited to, the following.

Internal controls matter more than ever. Even in the fast moving sectors such as blockchain, cryptoassets, and artificial intelligence, the reality remains that internal controls remain at least as important, if not more important, than in the eras the preceded these rapid technological evolutions. For example at FTX, it was discovered that confidential client information and data were stored and shared in unsecured Google Docs that were able to accessed by anyone within the organization. Additionally, the organization itself had no CFO, the Board of Directors was comprised mainly of people with personal or familial connection to the management of FTX, and had never undergone a comprehensive financial audit.[4] The passage of ASU 2023-08 following the collapse of FTX, while not directly connected to the firm itself, seemed to focus exclusively on more transparent and real-time reporting of cryptoassets versus reliance on traditional audit and attestation methods (FASB, 2023). Hindsight is always 20/20, but the fact remains that the internal control failures – while not leading to the fraud at FTX – allowed the fraud and those individuals conducting these frauds to escape notice and associated consequences for these actions until billions in investor damages had occurred.

Patchwork Reporting Standards Do Not Help. An ongoing issue that continues to prove an obstacle to wider adoption of tokenized assets and blockchain-based transactions is the patchwork of enforcement and legislation that has been passed across various jurisdictions. For example, the mainland Chinese market has virtually banned all cryptoassets from trading and being used within its borders, whereas the European Union has sought to establish leadership over the cryptoasset marketplace by creating laws and frameworks for others to follow, and the USA has seemingly been in a continuous state of flux when related to crypto legislation and frameworks.

[3]https://cointelegraph.com/news/tremors-from-ftx-s-collapse-reverberate-through-the-scientific-community

[4]https://www.breaches.cloud/incidents/ftx/#:~:text=MultiAccount%20Strategy%20%2D%20FTX%20primarily%20kept,assets.%E2%80%9D%20(pg%2028)

- Specifically, the back and forth that has accompanied cryptoassets with regards to how crypto is treated by financial regulators has – definitively – led to hesitation, slower allocations, and decreased investments overall by entrepreneurs in the space. This was particularly highlighted during the Biden Administration, where the regulatory landscape was defined by the antagonistic approach and regulation-by-enforcement angle embraced by the SEC. The re-election of Donald Trump to the White House has led to a pivot of regulation and oversight by the SEC, which while enthusiastically received by the industry has again led to a backlash in terms of investment options and funds.

Emphasizing technology over fundamentals. Here is where the mismatch between what the reality on the ground for cryptoassets is versus the reality for financial markets at large. Specifically, the bubble and froth that has accompanied cryptoassets has also occurred in multiple other industries over time, and in that sense, the implications are similar for both technological paradigms in the fact that business leaders can potentially over-focus on the technical specifics of the tools themselves versus the business applications of said tools (Luo & Yu, 2024). The ramifications of this course of action, colloquially known as shiny object syndrome, can be substantial not only for the individual firms impacted but also the crypto industry at large. By focusing exclusively on the technical aspects of a certain project versus the real-world or tangible business use cases, technology advocates risk over-exposing these implementations before they are ready for that level of scrutiny.

Heightened Risks Due to Crypto Centralization

One risk that began to emerge in 2025, both in terms of crypto-native organizations and TradFi institutions launching products and services in this space, is the risk of centralization of risk. While the likelihood of a CBDC remains unlikely, and even less likely with the re-election of Donald Trump to the White House, that particular aspect of centralization appears to be minimized. That said, the reality is that as cryptoassets and other on-chain information become increasingly integrated across various aspects of the economy the odds of some centralized risk will also accelerate and become more commonplace. Let's take a look at a few examples of how the positive trends of increased adoption and utilization of cryptoassets might also increase the risk of systemic danger to markets through cryptoassets.

Stablecoin development is centralized risk and reward for crypto investors.[5]

With the news that Circle conducted an IPO for 2025 generating increased enthusiasm and interest in the stablecoin sector the reality is that stablecoins are continuing to increase in importance during the year. With the combined market

[5]https://www.brookings.edu/articles/the-hidden-danger-of-re-centralization-in-blockchain-platforms/#:~:text=Similarly%2C%20MakerDAO's%20core%20decisions%20have,protocol%20governance%20and%20transaction%20processing

capitalization of stablecoins in excess of over $200 billion the odds of institutional investors coming into the space will only accelerate moving forward. Circle generated nearly $2 billion in revenue during 2024, and although profitability has declined year-over-year due to increased competition and other interest-rate related pressures, the interest in institutional stablecoins is going to increase as the potential for profits and earnings will accelerate.[6]

The public debut of a private stablecoin issuer, the first such event in the U.S. markets, is set to send shockwaves through both the cryptoasset sector as well as the wider financial markets. While Circle is the second largest such stablecoin, well behind the market capitalization of USDT (issued by Tether) it is well regarded as a financial instrument and option for stablecoins in the marketplace. Some of the implications of this debut, outside of the rather obvious implications for investors and users of USDC and Circle at large include, but are not limited to, the following.

- Income producing crypto is on the rise. With the rise of staking operations, alongside the proof-of-stake blockchain methodology that continues to assume a leadership position in the cryptoasset sector. One of the primary areas that has remained a work-in-progress versus a reality for many investors is the lack of income producing ability for crypto investors. Staking, by its nature, allows crypto investors to participate in the validation of blockchain transactions but also enables those investors an opportunity to benefit from such activities. With the potential of stablecoins becoming publicly traded, especially with Circle generating nearly $2 billion in revenue, this also creates an opportunity for potential distributions of earnings.
- Crypto audits must become a priority. As the size and scope of stablecoin issuers becomes more well known and understood by the wider marketplace it is also going to be that audits and audit-adjacent services become (1) better understood, (2) more transparent, and (3) more commonplace in the space (Jackson, 2023). While much progress has been made in this area, the reality remains that the majority of cryptoassets – including stablecoins such as USDT, have never undergone a comprehensive financial audit. Circle, to the contrary, has long been working toward improving financial reporting practices as well as conveying these findings to the marketplace. After the firm does goes public and must fulfill SEC reporting requirements – and address investor concerns on an ongoing basis – the priority placed on these topics will only increase.
- Crypto firms like Circle can diversify by expanding beyond stablecoins into areas such as decentralized finance (DeFi), asset tokenization, and cross-border payments. Building partnerships with traditional financial institutions can open access to new markets and regulatory clarity. Circle could also invest in blockchain infrastructure, offering tools for developers and enterprises.

[6]https://finance.yahoo.com/news/stablecoins-go-mainstream-after-circles-blockbuster-ipo-heres-what-they-do-152159324.html

Geographic diversification – targeting regions with growing crypto adoption – can reduce reliance on U.S. markets. Additionally, entering sectors like digital identity or compliance tech could create synergies with existing services. Diversification not only broadens revenue streams but also enhances resilience against market volatility and regulatory shifts, positioning Circle for long-term sustainable growth.

Even as the rise of dollar-backed stablecoins continues virtually unabated, there has also been consistent and strong pushback against the concept of a CBDC. While a CBDC may indirectly generate benefits for users and investors the fact is that these activities will not be universally cheered by the marketplace. Rather, the fact that these instruments could also be used for surveillance has played a significant part of the opposition that many such instruments have faced even as they technically become more realistic.

Central Bank Digital Currencies

Given the rapid growth and adoption of various cryptoassets by actors across the financial services landscape, it would seem reasonable to ask about how exactly these instruments are going to evolve and move forward. Stated simply, the outgrowth in the interest and investment in CBDCs can be summarized as follows; governments and other economic regions/blocs have seen the benefits of tokenized assets and transactions and want to leverage these upsides for their own benefit.

Prior to any further discussion or debate around the CBDC conversation, it is pertinent to point out that CBDCs do not – in a traditional sense – represent cryptoassets, nor the idea of decentralized crypto transactions. Rather, a CBDC should rather be thought of as a combination of existing payment rails, regulations, and rule, with certain selected aspects of blockchain-based payments. By integrating cryptoassets within the existing rules and frameworks that govern most – if not all – transactions in the current landscape, the centralized and control able to be exercised by issuers (governments) is difficult to overstate.

This is why, despite the growing interest in these financial instruments by individuals and institutions across the globe, there are substantial doubts regarding whether or not these developments are positive or negative news for both the crypto space and/or the wider financial markets space at large. For example, if the co-opting of crypto continues to evolve and become more mainstream, the questions of regulation and increased compliance requirements will invariably shift from less of an "if" question to more of a "when" question. Especially as private sector options continue to expand and develop new product and service offerings, the importance of consistent and standardized audit and attestation offerings will only increase in importance (Kanu, 2025).

Additionally, the rise of interest and investment in CBDCs also reflects the unfortunate increase scope creep of governments, and government agencies across the world. Put simply, following the global financial crisis of 2007–2008, and compounded yet again during the government responses to the COVID-19 virus, the role of government has seemingly been trending in one direction; expansion. Digitization of information, including the financial transactions that all individuals, entrepreneurs, and organizations engage with on a daily basis, can also be considered a megatrend that is trending in one direction. From governments taking direct ownership stakes in private sector enterprises, to price controls and mandates seemingly in vogue (although having failed spectacularly in the past), and general government meddling on the rise, the trend is clear.

Lastly, and something that will be expanded upon in the privacy discussion surrounding the potential implementation of CBDCs is that there is virtually no limit on the interest of leaders – government and corporate alike – to direct and influence certain behaviors among consumers, businesses, and members of the public. As has already been seen, via the implementation of social credit scores by the CCP, governments are actively seeking to take a more active role in the daily lives of those (citizens) who – on paper – are actually the ones in charge.

An additional driving force in the debate around the development and implementation of CBDCs is the reality that these instruments also serve as an existential risk to the current global reserve currency; the U.S. dollar. While the vast majority of privately issued stablecoins, for better worse, utilize the dollar for reserve purposes, the rise and potential spread of CBDCs need not follow this pattern. In fact, the reality that over 100 nations are working on versions of CBDCs would seem to indicate the opposite; the dollar is facing the greatest threat to its global reserve currency status ever. Whether it takes the form of authoritarian regimes wanting greater control over individuals and institutions, regimes seeking to develop a viable alternative to the petrodollar paradigm that has dominated global affairs for nearly 60 years, or nations with an alternative free of capitalism and market driven choices there are multiple threats and challenges to the status of both the dollar and the primacy of market-driven capitalism.

As the cryptoasset landscape continues to enter mainstream financial conversations, including the return of NFTs to levels last seen in 2021, reinforce the intersection currently underway between crypto, intellectual property, and AI. Given that, the need for comprehensive audit and confirmation practices for these different types of intellectual property will become more of a priority going forward. Mirroring the rising percentage of the value of publicly traded firms linked to intangible assets, the rising number and scope of intellectual property are creating an environment that will highlight the need for better accounting practices linked to these instruments (Hosseini Bamakan et al., 2023).

As tokenized assets continue to move into the financial mainstream, they're raising big questions for the world of accounting. These digital assets – including cryptocurrencies like bitcoin and ether, as well as stablecoins, NFTs, and tokenized securities – are built using blockchain technology and represent a wide range of ownership rights and claims. While they offer transparency, speed, and innovation, they don't fit neatly into the traditional accounting and reporting rules that businesses have relied on for decades. This disconnect is creating practical problems around how to record, measure, report, and audit these assets in a way that makes sense to regulators, investors, and auditors alike.

One of the first challenges companies face is figuring out how to classify tokenized assets on their books. Are they cash? Inventory? Financial instruments? Intangibles? The answer is: it depends. In the USA, the Financial Accounting Standards Board (FASB) recently released ASU 2023-08, which provides clearer rules for some crypto assets. Under this standard, certain types of crypto assets must be measured at fair value, with gains or losses going straight to earnings. But the rule doesn't cover everything. It excludes things like stablecoins, tokenized securities, and most NFTs. That leaves companies relying on older rules that weren't designed for digital assets. Depending on how the asset is used, it might be treated as an intangible, inventory, or a financial instrument – each with its own rules and implications. Without a standard approach, companies end up applying different policies, which makes it hard to compare financial statements across the industry.[7]

Valuing tokenized assets brings its own set of challenges. Crypto markets operate 24/7 and are notoriously volatile, which makes it difficult to pin down a consistent and accurate value at any given point in time. On top of that, prices for the same asset can vary significantly between exchanges. Companies have to make clear decisions about which pricing sources to use and how they'll apply those rules consistently. For some tokens – especially NFTs or thinly traded coins – there might not even be an active market, meaning firms have to rely on estimates and judgment. That bumps these assets into level 2 or level 3 of the fair value hierarchy, where inputs aren't always observable or verifiable. In short, assigning value to tokenized assets is more art than science and that makes auditors – and investors – nervous.

When it comes to presenting and disclosing tokenized assets in financial statements, the rules are still playing catch-up. Companies are expected to explain what these assets are, why they hold them, and how they value them – but there's no universal checklist. The best disclosures today include details about how the assets are used (as investments, for operations, or customer obligations), how they're valued, and whether they're held directly or by a third-party custodian. It's also important for companies to be transparent about any legal or regulatory risks associated with holding or using crypto assets. As investors become more curious – and cautious – about digital holdings, the pressure to provide clearer, more consistent disclosures will only increase.

Auditing tokenized assets is also proving to be a major hurdle. Unlike traditional assets, crypto doesn't come with bank statements or paper trails. Proving ownership often means verifying access to private keys and digital wallets, which requires specialized tools and expertise. If a company uses a third-party custodian, auditors need to review their security and control procedures as well. And as seen in recent high-profile failures like FTX, weak governance and missing internal controls can allow serious problems to go undetected. Companies that

---

[7]https://www.pillsburylaw.com/en/news-and-insights/digital-assets-regulated-us-elsewhere.html#:~:text=Under%20U.S.%20federal%20securities%20laws,expectation%20of%20profit%20by%20investors

deal with tokenized assets need to invest in strong internal controls, secure wallet management, and reliable transaction tracking. At the same time, the accounting profession is still developing standardized procedures for auditing crypto, leaving a lot of room for inconsistency and risk.[8]

Adding to all of this is the regulatory confusion that still surrounds tokenized assets. Different countries are taking very different approaches. The European Union has passed the MiCA regulation to create a consistent set of rules for crypto, but the USA remains fragmented, with agencies like the SEC and CFTC offering competing interpretations. This patchwork of laws makes life especially difficult for multinational companies trying to apply the same accounting treatment across jurisdictions. It also complicates tax reporting, compliance, and risk disclosures. For global businesses, understanding and managing the regulatory landscape is almost as challenging as the accounting itself.

In the end, the accounting and reporting challenges tied to tokenized assets reflect a broader issue: financial systems are struggling to keep up with the pace of digital innovation. The release of ASU 2023-08 is a step in the right direction, but much more work remains to be done – especially when it comes to stablecoins, NFTs, and tokenized versions of traditional securities. Accountants, regulators, and auditors need to work together to create frameworks that are both flexible enough to handle emerging technologies and rigorous enough to protect investors and uphold market integrity. Until that happens, companies dealing in tokenized assets will continue to face uncertainty – and so will the users of their financial statements.

Conclusion

Tokenized assets have progressed from fringe innovations to influential financial instruments with global relevance. As this chapter has shown, the journey from bitcoin's libertarian roots to institutional ETF offerings and government-sponsored digital currencies reflects a dramatic transformation in how value is created, stored, and transferred. Yet, the pace of regulatory, technological, and market developments has often outstripped accounting, reporting, and governance capabilities. Critical challenges – such as the lack of internal controls, fragmented legal frameworks, and inadequate audit standards – remain persistent barriers to trust and scalability. As adoption deepens and tokenization expands across sectors, strengthening accounting frameworks, regulatory clarity, and assurance mechanisms is essential to ensure transparency, accountability, and sustainable growth in the digital asset economy.

References

FASB. (2023, December 13). *FASB issues ASU 2023-08 on accounting for crypto assets.* Deloitte Heads Up.

[8]https://www.cpajournal.com/2025/03/24/auditing-cryptocurrency-companies/

Goble, J. M. (2025). *The future of digital assets and cryptocurrencies: Accounting standards and challenges*. SSRN. https://doi.org/10.2139/ssrn.5138691

Hosseini Bamakan, S. M., Nezhadsistani, N., Bodaghi, O., & Qu, Q. (2023). *Patents and intellectual property assets as non-fungible tokens: Key technologies and challenges*. arXiv.

International Monetary Fund. (2025). Tokenization and financial market inefficiencies. *IMF Economic Review*, *63*(1).

Jackson, T. (2023). Accounting for digital assets. *Accounting Auditing & Accountability Journal*.

Kanu, D. H. (2025, January 30). *Digital currencies financial reporting and auditing: A new concern for accounting professionals in the accounting industry*. SSRN. https://doi.org/10.2139/ssrn.5138691

Luo, M., & Yu, S. (2024). Financial reporting for cryptocurrency. *Review of Accounting Studies*, *29*(2), 1707–1740. https://doi.org/10.1007/s11142-022-09741-w

Chapter 5

Technology Changing the Accounting Business Model

Abstract

This chapter provides a concise overview of the evolving accounting landscape shaped by emerging technologies, with a particular focus on artificial intelligence (AI); environmental, social, and governance (ESG) reporting; tokenized assets; and automation. It highlights the expanding role of CPAs and financial professionals in delivering advisory services that go beyond technical expertise, emphasizing implementation support and strategic integration. Key themes include AI onboarding, ESG data governance, the financial implications of stablecoins, and the transition from traditional billing models to value-based pricing in response to automation. As technological change accelerates, professionals who adopt adaptive, client-centered approaches are well-positioned to lead the accounting profession into a new era.

Keywords: Innovation; accounting; financial reporting; artificial intelligence; automation

Introduction

Outside of the direct effects of these technological and reporting changes being implemented across the business landscape and marketplace, it is also worth noting that the rise of said forces and technological trends are going to create entirely new business lines and opportunities for CPAs and other financial professionals. Specifically, these opportunities will extend beyond simply understanding these technologies but will also include tactics and ways in which these professionals can offer advisory services to clients around the implementation and troubleshooting of these ideas over time.

Artificial Intelligence, ESG Investments and the Future of Tokenized Assets, 45–47

Published under exclusive licence by Emerald Publishing Limited
doi:10.1108/978-1-83708-108-020261005

AI. AI is perhaps the most discussed yet simultaneously the most misunderstood technological tool and paradigm shift that has made it to the mainstream financial conversation during the last decade. Arguably even more misunderstood than bitcoin and blockchain, which will be discussed in more detail below, AI also has to contend with the unfortunate reality that virtually every person who will come across AI in the workplace has been previously exposed to AI via mass media. This exposure can, and often does, lead to an overestimation of the capabilities of AI, underestimating the time and complexity of properly training and de-bugging AI applications, and the negative effect of these implementations on employee morale. As the profession seeks to redefine not only the present but also the future of itself, the need for profession-wide solutions to staffing, billing, and reputational issues must be assessed objectively, including those provided directly and indirectly via AI (Reilly, 2025).

Ways in which financial professionals can assist clients with AI onboarding include, but are not limited to, the following. First, conducting analytics to ascertain whether or not AI is an appropriate tool for the company in question is a reasonable place to start. Put simply, just because a company wants to integrate AI into operations does not mean that it is the correct fit for the problem at hand (Weinberg & Faccia, 2024). Second, and assuming that AI is determined to be the correct and appropriate tool for the company in question, conducting a review of internal controls and whether or not these controls are being followed or not is a logical next step in this process. Such questions will become more pointedly important as the evolution from traditional computing to quantum computing accelerates, amplifying already existing doubts and questions related to controls and workflow processes (Lazirko, 2023). Third, what oftentimes is important next is to conduct employee training and education programs to ensure that the employees whose tasks are going to be most impacted are aware of how these tools are going to change the tasks and job currently handled by employees.

ESG reporting. One of the largest fields of financial reporting and disclosures that will need to evolve and will multiple opportunities for financial professionals is how the actual reporting of ESG data will be handled (Pargmann & Berding, 2024). For example, and especially since the standards and reporting frameworks for these types of information remain very much a work in progress, the integration of AI and other advanced analytics into how these reports are created stand positioned to provide essential data and analytical capability moving forward.

Tokenized data. Cryptoassets have taken the financial reporting world by storm, and the implications of these changes are only set to accelerate moving forward. As discussed previously, the rise of stablecoins represents perhaps the most purpose built cryptocurrencies for the use as a medium of exchange. These purpose built tokens are continuing to drive adoption and utilization of crypto by both individuals and institutions but are also creating multiple obstacles for firms and taxpayers seeking to adapt these tools.

AI and automation. The most direct impact of AI and other kinds of automation on the accounting, tax, and auditing sectors has been the ability to perform more real-time analytics over data and to perform these analytics over a broader and deeper set of information. This can take the form of real-time tax analytics and reporting, more comprehensive audits and assurance procedures over organizational data, and the ability to create entirely new service lines for the firm in question. One aspect of this increasing automation that can oftentimes go overlooked is that as automation increases, and clients become more aware of the time savings involved with automation there will need to a revisiting as to how CPA firms bill and generate revenue.

Specifically, the concept of the billable hour looks increasingly outmoded in a business landscape where time savings and efficiency have become the proverbial name of the game. The changing nature of billing, influenced by technology as well as external pressures, will also lead to an altered firm structure and business model throughout the accounting industry (Rapoport, 2024). In this environment, where it costs less time to perform tasks, requires fewer individuals to do so, and the entire business landscape is aware of these facts it will be necessary for firms to shift to more of a value billing model to accurately reflect the realities of the work being performed.

Regardless of which specific area a CPA firm or financial professional is most interested in offering advisory services around the fact remains that the business landscape has continued to evolve and change on an almost daily basis, with the implications of these technological and reporting changes still unfolding. This is even more true for the accounting profession, as Gen Z is held up as both potential solution and potential amplifier of current pipeline and reputational obstacles facing the profession (Stubbington, 2025). No matter which company is being discussed, there are going to be changed enacted via new technologies, reporting frameworks, and analytics that are made available via these new reporting paradigms. Proactive and forward thinking professionals, as is almost always the case, will be able to generate opportunities and new revenue lines through seeking to address client problems and drive operational improvements.

References

Lazirko, M. (2023). Quantum computing standards & accounting information systems. arXiv. https://arxiv.org/abs/2311.11925

Pargmann, J., & Berding, F. (2024). Integrating sustainability in controlling and accounting practices: A critical review and implications for competences in German vocational business education. arXiv. https://arxiv.org/abs/2406.02314

Rapoport, M. (2024, April 30). Accounting firms rethink their ownership structure. *The Wall Street Journal*. https://www.wsj.com/articles/accounting-firms-rethink-their-ownership-structure-ccbd38c9

Reilly, R. (2025, January 22). Accounting profession-wide solutions to the talent shortage. *The CPA Journal*. https://www.cpajournal.com/2025/01/22/accounting-profession-wide-solutions-to-the-talent-shortage/

Stubbington, T. (2025, February 5). The Gen Z problem for audit firms. *Financial Times*. https://www.ft.com/content/3a98089b-977a-4c52-ab4f-656556dc2d6a

Weinberg, A. I., & Faccia, A. (2024). Transforming triple-entry accounting with machine learning: A path to enhanced transparency through analytics. arXiv. https://arxiv.org/abs/2411.15190

Chapter 6

Methods to Improve ESG Analytics

Abstract

Technological advancements and evolving reporting frameworks are reshaping the business landscape, presenting new advisory opportunities for CPAs and financial professionals. Artificial intelligence (AI), environmental, social, and governance (ESG) reporting, and tokenized assets are driving demand for expertise in implementation, governance, and compliance. CPAs can offer critical services such as AI readiness assessments, internal controls evaluation, and employee training. In ESG reporting, AI-enhanced analytics will support evolving disclosure requirements. The adoption of tokenized data and automation enables real-time financial insights but necessitates a shift from traditional billable-hour models to value-based billing. Proactive financial professionals can capitalize on these trends to drive innovation and client value.

Keywords: Artificial intelligence; ESG reporting; tokenized assets; automation; CPA advisory services; value-based billing

Introduction

Although the topics and conversations related to sustainability, sustainable investing, and broader topics related to green investing might have seemingly catapulted to public discourse only recently, the reality is that green investing has existed in a multitude of forms for decades. Detailed below are working definitions of how the sustainability discourse has evolved over time. One of the modern interpretations of sustainability investing has taken the form of the multiple capital model, which necessitated better and more comprehensive reporting of both financial and non-financial information (Sariyer et al., 2024). These multiple capitals include financial, manufactured, intellectual, human, social and relational, and

Artificial Intelligence, ESG Investments and the Future of Tokenized Assets, 49–56

Published under exclusive licence by Emerald Publishing Limited
doi:10.1108/978-1-83708-108-020261006

natural; these different types of capital reflect both the changing attitude toward business by external users of financial data and the improvement in tools that allow firms to report on a more comprehensive set of data.

The multiple capital model has grown out of a much wider, although less quantitative, mindset as to how firms should be evaluated by the stakeholder community (which includes but is not limited to financial investors), corporate social responsibility, and the stakeholder model of financial reporting. Stated simply, the concept underpinning the stakeholder theory of financial reporting is that corporations should adopt a broader lens as to how data are reported to creditors, investors, and regulators alike. Stakeholders, this theory holds, represent a much more diverse audience than just stockholders. Therefore, an organization's aim should be to satisfy the needs and expectations of this broader stakeholder base. The multiple capital model quantified these expectations and ultimately led to the launch of integrated financial reporting.

ESG, by all objective measures, represents issues and topics that, at the very least, are deserving of further analysis and examination, while acknowledging the reality that some of these investments have fallen victim to greenwashing and other such pitfalls. AI has rapidly moved from a conceptual conversation and topic, to one that continues to dominate both the headlines and investors conversation.

Generally speaking, there are several ways in which AI can deliver value to the ESG and sustainable investing space. While these areas are expanded upon below, a few general themes are addressed by way of context.

- *Improved transparency*: One of the largest issues surrounding ESG investing is the lack of transparency and consistency with regards to the reporting and communicating of ESG initiative results. Specifically, the lack of consistent and standardized communication and reporting can also lead to accusations of greenwashing and other ESG initiatives that are not as comprehensive as advertised. Greenwashing and other related problems continue to prove to be challenging obstacles for sustainability-related projects and initiatives launching into the marketplace. Leveraging AI to collect and examine both quantitative and qualitative information is perhaps the most obvious and straight-forward use case for AI in this sector.
- *Real-time adjustments*: As sustainability projects and ESG initiatives continue to focus on both improving financial outcomes and meeting goals that are connected to the ESG ethos, the reality is that these projects will need to evolve over time. Specifically, as it connects to projects such as green bonds, depending on how these bonds are structured by the issuing entity, it might result in variable payments and other reporting metrics. The analytic capability of AI programs can allow bonds and bond issuers to make said adjustments on an on-demand basis, especially as ESG projects face increasing expectations and demand from investors and stakeholders (Brozini et al., 2023).
- *On-demand comparisons*: Another significant issue that can prove challenging for organizations seeking to implement more comprehensive ESG projects is that many of these initiatives do not have peer projects or items that are comparable on a real-time basis. AI can certainly help not only in the analytics of

certain specific projects but also to deliver value in the ability of organizations to model and test an array of scenarios.

There are also additional ways in which the implementation of AI within an ESG framework can deliver value both on a project-by-project basis and at the organization at large. Generally speaking, AI can provide deeper and more real-time insights, help develop more efficient processes, and add transparency to the decision-making process that takes place within an organization (Reuters, 2024). These advances and methods of assistance can help create more sustainable and responsible business practices. Other ways that AI can deliver quantifiable benefits include, but are not limited to, the following:

1. *Environmental analytics and predictive reporting*: AI can make use of its processing power to analyze large quantities of environmental data, which in turn can help create an assessment of firms' environmental impact. Specific analyzable items include a given firm's carbon footprint, energy usage, waste management practices, and water conservation and recycling. AI algorithms can also help predict future trends and impacts, assisting with the longer-term planning and strategic capital allocation processes at the firm.
2. *Social action and impact assessments*: An AI program can help evaluate the social impact of companies, on both an internal and external basis, including the collection and reporting of data connected to diversity and inclusion efforts. AI bots can also collect and analyze large amounts of social media information, which can aid management in gauging public sentiment as well as employee satisfaction.
3. *Governance reporting*: AI programs can also streamline the monitoring of governance standards and regulatory compliance on a number of different issues. Specifically, the program can help track changes in regulations, improve compliance with ethical standards and best practices, as well as identify potential risks of breaches related to governance issues.
4. *Risk assessment*: AI programs can also evaluate risks that are specific to ESG-related activities which can be both qualitative and quantitative in nature. This is of special importance as the ESG-related marketplace has continued to grow in size and scope while also increasingly finding itself under growing investor scrutiny. Given the business, reputational, and political risks that ESG and green investing can incur (such as political backlash or divestment), a robust risk assessment and reporting process represents an area within which AI can assist financial and managerial professionals.

While green bonds might be the most obvious place where AI can improve the reporting and transparency of the project in question, there are other areas in which AI can be of value for sustainability and ESG initiatives.

1. *AI for climate predictions and weather modelling*: Companies such as IBM and startups working with established technology firms are using AI to enhance climate prediction models and weather forecasting. This can help mitigate

the effect of climate change, dramatic weather events, and offset some of the damages caused by natural disasters.

2. *AI leverage for sustainable agriculture*: Various AI tools and technologies are being used to optimize farming practices, reduce waste, and increase crop yield. An example of these applications includes Microsoft's deployment of the AI for Earth program that assists farmers monitoring crop health, soil quality, and water usage. By improving these metrics, farmers and the farming supply chain can improve sustainability throughout the supply chain.
3. *Energy usage and optimization*: AI is also being used to optimize energy efficiency and usage in both buildings and industrial operations. For instance, the DeepMind AI out of Google helped reduce energy consumption for cooling its data centers by 40% by using AI-driven management system. If and when these practices are replicated across different energy sectors, it could lead to wholescale energy reduction for increasingly important data centers going forward.
4. *Improving supply chain ethics*: As unusual as it might seem, the implementation of AI can also help improve the ethics of supply chains. Specifically, firms like IBM and use AI alongside other tools to track and verify the sustainability and ethical sourcing or products at all points of the supply chains.

One specific example of how AI can be used by private market actors to create quantifiable business benefits is how the Spanish multinational power and energy company Iberdrola used IBM. Iberdrola is a leading producer of wind power, as well as being known for its additional investments and positions in renewable energy. Iberdrola has adopted AI throughout the scope of its operations, including but not limited to the following use cases:

1. *Renewable energy production and management*: By leveraging IBM's AI and data analytic capabilities embedded therein, Iberdrola optimizes the operation and maintenance of its renewable energy assets. These applications include managing predictive maintenance of wind turbines and other sustainable energy assets such as solar panels. On top of maintenance management, AI also allows Iberdrola to collect and analyze data in real time from sensors and predict potential faults of inefficiencies.
2. *Smart grid integration*: Iberdrola has also been working on various smart grid initiatives in which IBM's AI and analytics solutions play a significant role in managing grid operations, improving energy distribution, and integrating renewable energy sources and assets more effectively. This is also a demonstrable way in which AI can enable further investment and deployment of new-level ESG initiatives.
3. *AI-enhanced customer service*: Iberdrola has also made use of IBM's AI to improve customer service operations, feedback, engagement, and the ability to deliver real-time support services. Specifically, this integration has allowed the use of an AI-driven chatbot and improved analytics.

There are also multiple use cases for how organizations can use (have already used) AI to improve supply chain transparency. Transparency, especially as it pertains to supply chains and supply chain management, is not as straight-forward a process as might have traditionally been the case. One notable example of a firm that has done just this is Everledger, which has integrated AI to not only improve the transparency of its supply chain but to also track and protect valuable items and inventory.

Everledger is also an example of an organization that had been able to effectively leverage and make use of an array of emerging technologies such as blockchain to augment and increase the effectiveness of AI for supply chains (Everledger, 2023). Specifically use cases such that could benefit from such additional transparency include gemstones and fine wine/spirits, where provenance and traceability play a large role in the valuation and market reputation of these products. There are several ways in which AI can help address the major issues that, while directly connected to precious gems, have implications across various industry lines. Specific to the diamond industry, Everledger had already implemented AI-based solutions in the following ways:

1. *Improving traceability and provenance*: A major issue in the diamond trade is the provenance of the precious gems as they move throughout the supply chain from point of origin to the final customer. Everledger's AI platform tracks the lifecycle of each diamond from the mine to help ensure that the stones are ethically sourced and not from conflict zones (so called blood diamonds).
2. *Reducing fraud*: A major issue the diamond market, as well as other gemstone, antique, and high-value asset markets, is fraud and counterfeiting. By combining the transparency of blockchain with the real-time analytical capability of AI, Everledger can help dramatically reduce the likelihood of frauds and other counterfeiting activities.
3. *Better ethics and sustainability*: By using AI, Everledger can not only increase the transparency and sustainability of its own supply chain, but it can also indirectly influence the traceability and transparency of supply chain partners as well.

While Everledger is no longer in business itself, the reality of integrating blockchain with AI within an industry that has long faced problems and issues with provenance and supply chain issues should be viewed as an example for other firms to follow going forward. Let's take a look at another case study example of how even a mid-size organization has effectively leveraged AI for green bond issuance and activities.

Amper Group: How a Mid-cap Defense-to-digital Firm Used AI to Bring ESG Bonds to Market

The sustainable-debt market keeps smashing records – more than $9 trillion in cumulative green, social, and sustainability bonds were outstanding by the end of 2024, and analysts at RBC Capital Markets expect another trillion dollars in issuance this year. One of the five themes they highlight for 2025 is "artificial intelligence as a net positive for decarbonization," noting that better data and faster analytics are making it easier for issuers and investors to prove real-world impact.

Against that backdrop, Spain-based Amper Group decided to refinance and expand its energy-transition business lines – micro-grids, coastal wind assets, and secure communications for renewable-powered defense installations – through sustainability-linked bonds (SLBs). Amper is a 3,800-employee, €427 million-revenue company with operations in more than 20 countries; as a mid-cap, it lacks the in-house ESG analytics teams that large banks enjoy. That resource gap pushed the firm to look for an external, automated solution that could satisfy both Spain's MARF exchange requirements and increasingly data-hungry institutional investors.

Building the Funding Program

With counsel from Cuatrecasas, Amper registered a €100 million SLB program on the Spanish Alternative Fixed-Income Market (MARF) in mid-2024. The framework aligns coupon step-ups with emissions-intensity reductions across Amper's energy-and-sustainability business unit as well as diversity targets for its defense division. The first tranche – €30.7 million of five-year notes priced at 8.5% – closed in July 2024 and is callable in 2027.

Injecting AI into ESG Verification

To convince investors that its key performance indicators (KPIs) were material, measurable, and on track, Amper turned to Clarity AI's ESG Risk Scoring platform. The cloud-based tool scrapes and standardizes over two million data points per day across 35,000 public and private companies, applying natural-language processing and machine-learning models trained on SASB, GRI, and SFDR taxonomies. In Amper's case, the platform produced a real-time ESG risk score of 73/100, well above its peer average, and flagged leading indicators – renewable-energy share, cyber-resilience posture, supplier-diversity ratios – that could be updated quarterly and automatically fed into MARF disclosures.

The AI layer solved three pain points common to mid-sized issuers:

- *Speed*: Traditional second-party opinions can take 8–12 weeks; Clarity AI's onboarding and scoring process took under a month.
- *Granularity*: Instead of a single letter grade, investors saw sub-scores (e.g., 93/100 in environmental management, 73/100 in social capital) with confidence intervals generated by the model.
- *Auditability*: Every metric was linked to an underlying data source, creating a transparent "data lineage" that auditors – and rating agencies – could trace.

Market Reception and Metrics of Success

On the back of the AI-enhanced disclosure package, Amper's debut bonds obtained a BBB-investment-grade rating from Ethifinance, rare for an SME-sized issuer in Spain, and attracted a geographically diverse order book led by Nordic impact funds and French insurers. The company has since tapped the program twice more, bringing total proceeds to €42.7 million, and management says coupon step-ups tied to its KPI glidepath are on track to save roughly 35 basis points relative to a vanilla bond of similar tenor.

Why the AI Angle Matters

1. *Credibility in a scrutinized market*: The International Capital Market Association's updated SLB Principles (June 2024) emphasize KPIs that are "core, relevant, and benchmarkable." AI-driven scoring helped Amper defend KPI selection during due-diligence calls, reducing investor skepticism about greenwashing.
2. *Regulatory readiness*: Europe's forthcoming Green Bond Standard will mandate pre- and post-issuance reporting that most mid-caps find resource-intensive. Automated data feed position Amper to comply without building a new internal reporting team.
3. *Portfolio integration for investors*: Asset managers that already consume Clarity AI data could drop Amper's bonds into ESG funds without customizing their screening models, widening the potential buyer base.

Challenges and Caveats

Amper's experience also highlights limitations. AI algorithms are only as good as the raw data they ingest; in emerging markets where suppliers don't report granular emissions, model confidence intervals widen. Moreover, the surge in SLBs has sparked debate on step-up materiality – if coupon penalties are small, the instrument's incentive effect may be weak. Finally, AI processing itself consumes energy; clarity AI reports that each full portfolio run emits roughly 0.8 kg of CO_2-equivalent. While trivial per bond, the footprint underscores a broader industry tension RBC flags: AI can be both a decarbonization enabler and a power-hungry disruptor.

Lessons for Other Issuers

- Leverage external AI platforms instead of building proprietary models; the plug-and-play approach accelerates time-to-market and satisfies investor transparency demands.
- Align AI outputs with recognized frameworks (SASB, GRI, SFDR, SLBP) to avoid "model-washing" accusations.

- Quantify cost of capital benefits – Amper estimates its AI-backed SLBs saved 35–45 bps versus a conventional issue, easily covering platform subscription fees.
- Prepare for continuous monitoring. AI scores update in near-real-time, so issuers must be ready to course-correct quickly if KPIs drift off track.

The Bottom Line

Amper's journey shows that sophisticated, AI-driven ESG analytics are no longer the sole province of global banks. By coupling a credible sustainability-linked framework with machine-learning-powered data, the company tapped a deeper capital pool, secured investment-grade pricing, and set itself up for forthcoming European reporting rules – all while channeling funds to tangible decarbonization projects. As AI tools mature and regulatory scrutiny tightens, the "Amper playbook" offers a template for mid-sized corporates worldwide looking to unlock green financing without blowing out their treasury budgets.

The integration of AI into ESG analytics marks a critical evolution in sustainable finance and corporate reporting. As demonstrated through frameworks like the multiple capital model and the Amper Group case study, AI enhances transparency, efficiency, and credibility in ESG initiatives. It enables real-time monitoring, data standardization, and investor assurance while supporting compliance with emerging global standards. However, the effectiveness of AI is contingent upon data quality, ethical deployment, and thoughtful alignment with material stakeholder concerns. Financial professionals who proactively adopt AI-driven ESG tools are uniquely positioned to lead in a market increasingly shaped by sustainability, accountability, and innovation.[1]

References

Bronzini, M., Nicolini, C., Lepri, B., Passerini, A., & Staiano, J. (2023, October 9). *Glitter or gold? Deriving structured insights from sustainability reports via large language models*. arXiv. https://arxiv.org/abs/2310.05628

Reuters Events. (2024, May 10). *Sustainability professionals using AI to help meet new reporting rules*. Reuters Events Sustainability Reporting and Data Management Survey.

Sariyer, G., Kumar Mangla, S., Chowdhury, S., Erkan Sozen, M., & Kazancoglu, Y. (2024). Predictive and prescriptive analytics for ESG performance evaluation: A case of Fortune 500 companies. *Journal of Business Research, 181*, 114742. https://doi.org/10.1016/j.jbusres.2024.114742

[1]https://www.nasdaq.com/articles/amper-sa-expands-bond-issuance-secure-financing
https://www.grupoamper.com/en/news/clarity-ai-supports-amper-in-enhancing-sustainability-practices-through-esg-risk-scoring/
https://www.grupoamper.com/wp-content/uploads/2024/06/Approval-of-Ampers-Board-to-register-a-Bond-Programme.pdf

Chapter 7

Integrating AI into Financial Markets

Abstract

The U.S. Stargate Project – a $500 billion AI infrastructure initiative – signals a global race for AI dominance. This initiative, paired with the growing convergence of AI, blockchain, and financial technologies, is reshaping capital markets, payment systems, and central bank strategies. Innovations like zero-day settlement, Project Hamilton, and SWIFT's blockchain efforts highlight the trend. Meanwhile, agentic AI introduces autonomous decision making and new ethical risks in areas like credit and trading. Major financial institutions are integrating GenAI to enhance customer service, compliance, and market intelligence. However, the shift raises systemic risk concerns, demanding transparency, robust oversight, and thoughtful governance.

Keywords: Stargate Project; GenAI in financial services; blockchain integration; agentic AI; systemic risk; zero-day settlement

On January 21, 2025, President Donald Trump announced the launch of the Stargate Project, a monumental artificial intelligence (AI) infrastructure initiative in the USA. This joint venture involves key industry players: OpenAI, SoftBank, Oracle, and MGX. The project is set to commence with an initial investment of $100 billion, with plans to scale up to $500 billion over the next four years. At this point, although the specifics of the project have unfortunately become mired in political and personal conflicts, it is worth revisiting both the impact of this specific project and the implications for the AI sector at large.[1]

---

[1]https://www.forbes.com/sites/moorinsights/2025/01/30/the-stargate-project-trump-touts-500-billion-bid-for-ai-dominance/

Artificial Intelligence, ESG Investments and the Future of Tokenized Assets, 57–65

Published under exclusive licence by Emerald Publishing Limited
doi:10.1108/978-1-83708-108-020261007

Objectives and Scope

The primary goal of the Stargate Project is to construct extensive data centers and virtual infrastructure to support the next generation of AI advancements. The initiative aims to alleviate current bottlenecks in data center capacity, which are essential for training and operating advanced AI models. By enhancing this infrastructure, the project seeks to position U.S. companies to compete more effectively on the global stage, particularly against nations like China.

Economic and Employment Impact

A significant aspect of the Stargate Project is its potential to stimulate the U.S. economy. The venture is expected to create approximately 100,000 jobs immediately, contributing to the reindustrialization of the country. These employment opportunities span various sectors, including construction, technology, and operations, thereby fostering economic growth and stability.

Strategic Partnerships and Roles

In this collaboration, SoftBank assumes financial responsibility, while OpenAI takes on operational duties. Masayoshi Son, CEO of SoftBank, will serve as the chairman of the joint venture. Other significant investors and partners include MGX and Oracle, with technology partnerships involving Arm, Microsoft, and Nvidia. These collaborations bring together a wealth of expertise and resources, underscoring a united effort to expand AI capabilities and infrastructure within the USA.[2]

Infrastructure Development

The project's initial phase includes the construction of a data center in Abilene, Texas, with plans to expand into other states. This development is crucial for providing the necessary infrastructure to train and run new AI models, addressing the current limitations in data center capacity. The expansion is expected to support the growing computational demands of AI technologies, facilitating advancements in various applications.

Healthcare Advancements

Beyond economic and technological benefits, the Stargate Project holds promise for significant advancements in healthcare. By leveraging AI capabilities, the initiative aims to improve disease detection and treatment, including early cancer detection and the development of personalized mRNA vaccines. These advancements have the potential to revolutionize healthcare delivery and outcomes, offering more precise and effective medical interventions.

---

[2]https://group.softbank/en/news/press/20250122

National Security and Technological Leadership

The Stargate Project is also viewed as a strategic move to bolster national security and ensure technological leadership. By investing heavily in AI infrastructure, the USA aims to maintain a competitive edge in technological innovation, safeguarding its interests and those of its allies. This initiative reflects a commitment to leading in the AI sector, addressing both economic and security considerations.

The Stargate Project represents a transformative investment in the USA's AI infrastructure, with far-reaching implications for the economy, healthcare, and national security. By uniting leading technology companies and committing substantial resources, this initiative aims to pave the way for significant advancements in AI, positioning the USA at the forefront of global technological innovation.

The pivot by the USA, mirroring investments and actions taken by other nations across the world, reflects the realization that AI will become a primary tool and component of business, policy, and investing decisions moving forward (Zhang et al., 2023). While AI and automation have existed in the accounting and financial services space for decades (to some extent), the pace and breadth of improvements that have been generated more recently stand to revolutionize how capital is allocated, policies and written and reviewed, and how these decisions are implemented.

It is true that AI, automated, other algorithmic trading methodologies have been utilized by major Wall Street banks and asset managers for decades, but the continued development and improvement of AI models, particularly GenAI models, represents a leap forward in the capabilities of AI for financial modeling, trading, and asset management. Let's examine a few of the more straight forward ways in which GenAI will continue to redefine financial markets over the coming year.

Zero-day Settlement Trading

One of the most persistent legacies of pre-internet and pre-highspeed trading is the simple fact that trades, transfers, and other movements of capital can take multiple days to settle. This is also where the retail and institutional implementations of AI are going to vary significantly, as from a retail perspective the instantaneous nature of transactions and data transfers is already present. Under the surface and retail user experience, however, the financial plumbing and methods by which data and financial information are transferred are in needs of substantive updates. Such a statement is not just the opinions technologically oriented individuals but has illustrated by actions taken by leading financial institutions in both the USA and across the globe.

As agentic AI becomes more mainstream and widely adopted by individuals and institutions alike another concept that will need to come to the forefront include how AI tools will be able to overlap and integrate blockchain and other emerging technologies within operations (Li et al., 2023). Several major projects have either been announced and implemented with AI and blockchain/tokenized assets or are coming to market in relatively short order. Let's take a look at one of the most prominent ones in question; Project Hamilton.

Project Hamilton

Project Hamilton was a collaborative research initiative launched in 2020 by the Federal Reserve Bank of Boston and the Massachusetts Institute of Technology's Digital Currency Initiative (MIT DCI). The project focuses on exploring the design and potential implementation of a U.S. central bank digital currency (CBDC). Its primary goal is to investigate how a CBDC could operate in a secure, scalable, and efficient manner to support the needs of the U.S. financial system.

Phase 1 of Project Hamilton concentrated on developing a high-performance transaction processor capable of handling a high volume of payments. Researchers created an open-source system, dubbed "OpenCBDC," that demonstrated the ability to process up to 1.7 million transactions per second while maintaining strong privacy protections and resilience against cyber threats.

Phase 2 expanded on this foundation by exploring additional features such as programmability, interoperability, and offline functionality. The project has emphasized transparency and open collaboration by releasing its findings and code to the public. Project Hamilton is not an active proposal to issue a CBDC but serves as a vital research effort to inform policymakers about the technological and operational considerations of digital currencies. It highlights the potential role of technology in modernizing monetary systems.

SWIFT

SWIFT (Society for Worldwide Interbank Financial Telecommunication) has been actively exploring the integration of blockchain technology to enhance global financial transactions. Recognizing blockchain's potential to improve efficiency, transparency, and security in cross-border payments, SWIFT has initiated several projects and partnerships aimed at modernizing its infrastructure.

One of its key efforts is the gpi (Global Payments Innovation) initiative, which incorporates elements of blockchain to provide faster, more transparent, and traceable international payments. SWIFT gpi enables real-time tracking of transactions and has been adopted by thousands of banks globally, laying a foundation for blockchain-like capabilities.

In collaboration with leading blockchain firms like Chainlink and R3, SWIFT has tested blockchain-based systems for facilitating secure communication and interoperability between various financial institutions and digital asset platforms. A notable project includes leveraging Chainlink's cross-chain interoperability protocol to explore tokenized asset transfers, ensuring seamless communication across different blockchain networks.

SWIFT has also conducted experiments to assess the viability of CBDCs within its network, aiming to create a unified system that bridges traditional banking with emerging digital currencies. These initiatives reflect SWIFT's commitment to maintaining its relevance in a rapidly evolving financial landscape by integrating blockchain's benefits while preserving the reliability of its global network.

It is interesting to note that both of these efforts, at least partially, required the intersection between blockchain and AI to function as advertised. It is also worth noting that much of the promise and excitement around AI adoption in terms of improvements and efficiencies will – by default – require a trustworthy source of data that can be relied upon to not only be accurate but also not be able to alter by nefarious actors. This is where the almost immutable nature of blockchain can play an important role in allowing the decisions made by AI applications to be trusted.

Potential Instability and Systemic Risks

One of the largest risks that automation in any form, but especially automation driven by AI, bots, or other algorithmic trading protocols can is that of transforming asymmetric risks to systemic risks, especially if these automated trading practices need to be subsequently audited (Hillebran et al., 2023). While this might sounds like a radical scenario, especially given the massive amounts of investment and interest that have poured into the AI and GenAI sectors, but a parallel event has occurred within the last years. As a result of a booming housing market banks, financial institutions, and asset managers alike become enamored with a new type of securitized instrument; collateralized debt obligations. The working theory behind these instruments was as follows; since housing prices were considered to be both stable and set to continue increasing in nature, these underlying assets were to serve as a solid basis for securitized products.

Such an arrangement worked perfectly fine until something that should have been relatively easy to foresee but was not occurred; housing prices dropped. Following the dramatic and widespread collapse in housing prices, these lower prices caused the securities upon which these were based to enter a downward spiral. The end effect of these building declining price spirals eventually led to one of the largest real estate collapses and economic recessions in U.S. history. As AI and automation, including GenAI algorithms that learn based on patterns and pattern recognition and apply these lessons to the marketplace, become more widespread, the likelihood of systemic risk continues to increase (Ming, 2024).

For example, in a marketplace, there are always higher risk and lower risk activities, trades, and investment strategies. Given regular conditions, and assuming a normal distribution of events and actions, there will always be a smaller amount of investors or activities at the lower risk end versus the mid-range tactics or ideas. If, however, market actors (investors) grow to view certain actions, investments, or activities as low risk on a universal basis, this will result in a concentration risk in these allegedly low-risk activities. In addition to the concentration of risk, this also means that the ability of firms to exit these holdings or investments without significant losses upon dissolution drop in value decreases as well. Such a scenario is exceedingly possible as virtually every investment firm or banking institution is seeking to implement and integrate AI across operations both internal and external to the firm.

Agentic AI

As AI continues to evolve and develop, a new subset of AI has moved into the mainstream conversation; agentic AI. This refers to an AI system that can demonstrate autonomy in actions, decision-making, and problem-solving capabilities. Such systems are designed to perform tasks without requiring constant human input or supervision (Wu et al., 2024). Specifically, the agentic terminology implies that these AI applications can act as an agent, meaning it can assist the environment, make decisions, and execute actions to achieve specific goals and/or outcomes. While every AI application, including agentic tools, will operate differently and posses varied characteristics, there are commonalities that exist across these tools. These include, but not are not limited to, the following:

- *Autonomy*: Agentic AI applications can operate independently, including the ability to make decisions and taking actions without direct intervention.
- *Goal-focused behaviour*: Agentic AI bots and applications work toward achieving predefined objectives and can update or adapt methods based on changing circumstances and data sets.
- *Perceptive and adaptive*: Agentic AI can sense, interpret, and respond to changes in the business environment, operating environment, or other data-related subsets of information.
- *Learning and iterative*: Agentic AI can incorporate machine-learning techniques to improve performance over time, refine decision-making criteria, and apply these updated learning models across different data sets.

The rise of agentic AI – machines that can make decisions and take actions on their own – presents a fascinating but deeply complex ethical puzzle. Let's be real: when something goes wrong, who's to blame? Is it the developers who coded the system, the company deploying it, or – wild as it sounds – the AI itself? This gray area leaves regulators scrambling to figure out how to assign accountability in a world where lines are increasingly blurred.

Then there's the issue of bias. Agentic AI learns from the data we feed it, and let's face it, data often reflect societal flaws. If the system is trained on biased information, it might unknowingly make discriminatory decisions, whether it's denying a loan or skewing hiring practices. That's a slippery slope no one wants to go down.

And privacy? Forget about it. These systems thrive on hoovering up mountains of personal data to operate, raising major red flags about how our information is being used – or misused.

The kicker? If agentic AI's objectives don't align with human values, we could be in trouble. Imagine a system that optimizes for speed or efficiency but disregards ethical considerations. The solution? Transparent development, robust safeguards, and a serious conversation about where we draw the line.

This is also an area where, especially as it pertains to the allocation of capital or granting of credit, that internal biases that are in place at the institution need to be safeguarded and mitigated against. How this will play out will be different from firm to firm, but each and every decision that is made – even partially – by AI or agentic AI must first be tested and examined to ensure that it is happening in an ethical and objective manner. For example, if the credit granting process normally involves the review of personally identifiable information as part of the review itself, what guardrails are in place to ensure the anonymity of these individuals? Even if this information and data is normally kept siloed when an individual is involved with the task, delegating this task to agentic AI can result in an inadvertent breaking down of these internal firewalls.

Examples

While agentic AI certainly represents a step forward in the ability of Aito be useful in the workforce via its ability to adapt and iterative decision making and problem solving tactics overtime, these bots do raise issues connected to ethics, the requirements of human oversight, and the remedies that will need to be created to address the odds.

Generative AI is rapidly moving from pilot projects to production-grade applications at the world's largest banks and market-data providers. Citigroup has launched two internal tools – Citi Assist and Citi Stylus – that guide employees through complex policies and instantly summarize lengthy documents, raising productivity across human resources, risk, compliance, and finance teams. Goldman Sachs, meanwhile, has introduced the GS AI Platform, an environment that brings together state-of-the-art large language models such as GPT-4 and Gemini to streamline document analysis, support investment-banking deal flow, and accelerate software development. JPMorgan Chase is similarly innovating with IndexGPT, a service built on GPT-4 that parses enormous data sets to design thematic investment strategies and help clients make better-informed portfolio decisions. Morgan Stanley has deployed the AI @ Morgan Stanley Assistant, a generative-AI chatbot that gives financial advisers on-demand access to the firm's intellectual capital, enriching interactions with high-net-worth clients. Finally, Bloomberg has engineered BloombergGPT, a domain-specific language model trained on vast troves of market text to generate news stories, analytical reports, and user-tailored insights for professional terminals.[3]

Beyond these flagship initiatives, generative AI is reshaping key operational functions across the industry. Virtual assistants now handle front-line customer queries, delivering instantaneous, context-aware responses that lift satisfaction scores while reducing call-center volumes. Compliance teams use GenAI models to monitor transactions continuously, surface anomalies, and document regulatory interpretations, thereby lowering the risk of enforcement actions. Finance departments are automating narrative sections of statutory and management reports, freeing analysts to focus on judgment-intensive tasks and improving

[3]https://www.reuters.com/technology/artificial-intelligence/citigroup-rolls-out-artificial-intelligence-tools-employees-eight-countries-2024-12-04/#:~:text=Citi%20Assist%20searches%20internal%20bank,Chief%20Operating%20Officer%20Anand%20Selva

overall accuracy. Market-research desks employ large language models to scan unstructured data, detect emerging trends, and generate concise strategy papers that feed directly into trading and investment decisions.

Taken together, these deployments underscore the transformative power of generative AI in financial services. Institutions that embed the technology deeply into workflows are already realizing tangible gains in efficiency, risk management, and client engagement – advantages that will compound as models grow more capable and data governance practices mature.

Several additional financial institutions are making significant strides in deploying AI to streamline operations and deliver smarter financial services.

Bank of America has been a leader in integrating AI into its client-facing operations. Its virtual assistant, *Erica*, has become one of the most widely used AI tools in retail banking. Built into the bank's mobile app, Erica helps millions of customers perform everyday banking tasks, such as tracking spending, monitoring credit scores, and navigating transaction disputes. Beyond customer service, Erica's machine-learning capabilities continue to improve, offering users increasingly personalized financial insights based on behavioral patterns and account activity.

HSBC has embedded AI into its anti-money laundering and fraud detection systems. By leveraging machine-learning algorithms that adapt to evolving criminal behavior, the bank has reduced false positives in transaction monitoring and strengthened its ability to detect suspicious activity in real time. The AI systems can identify anomalies across billions of transactions, helping compliance teams focus on higher-risk events while improving response times and regulatory adherence.

Wells Fargo has focused on using AI to enhance back-office efficiency and internal decision making. Through its AI Enterprise Solutions group, the bank has implemented natural language processing tools to analyze customer feedback and detect emerging issues. Additionally, the firm uses AI to optimize loan underwriting models, assessing creditworthiness by evaluating a broader range of variables, including real-time income data and spending behavior. This has allowed for more inclusive lending practices while managing portfolio risk more effectively.

Conclusion

This chapter explores the accelerating integration of AI into financial markets, catalyzed by initiatives like the U.S. Stargate Project and the convergence of AI with blockchain and digital assets. Emerging technologies such as zero-day settlement, Project Hamilton, and SWIFT's blockchain modernization exemplify this trend. The rise of agentic AI introduces autonomous decision-making capabilities, raising ethical, regulatory, and systemic risk concerns. Major financial institutions are operationalizing GenAI for compliance, reporting, trading, and client services. While these advances promise efficiency and innovation, they necessitate robust oversight, data integrity, and ethical governance to mitigate concentration risks and ensure stability in evolving financial systems.

References

Hillebrand, L., Berger, A., Deußer, T., Dilmaghani, T., Khaled, M., Kliem, B., Loitz, R., Pielka, M., Leonhard, D., Bauckhage, C., & Sifa, R. (2023). *Improving zero-shot text matching for financial auditing with large language models*. arXiv. https://doi.org/10.48550/arXiv.2308.06111

Li, Y., Wang, S., Ding, H., & Chen, H. (2023). *Large language models in finance: A survey*. arXiv. https://doi.org/10.48550/arXiv.2311.10723

Ming, J. (2024). *StockAgent: AI agents for financial market trading*. arXiv. https://doi.org/10.48550/arXiv.2407.18957

Wu, H., Yao, Q., Liu, Z., Huang, B., Zhuang, Y., Tang, H., & Liu, E. (2024). *Blockchain for finance: A survey*. arXiv. https://doi.org/10.48550/arXiv.2402.17219

Zhang, B., Yang, H., Zhou, T., Babar, A., & Liu, X.-Y. (2023). *Enhancing financial sentiment analysis via retrieval-augmented large language models*. arXiv. https://doi.org/10.48550/arXiv.2310.04027

Chapter 8

Tokenized Financial Markets

Abstract

The approval of spot Bitcoin and Ether ETFs in 2024 has accelerated interest in tokenization across financial markets, with potential growth estimated at $10 trillion. Key developments include stablecoins, DeFi, staking, artificial intelligence (AI)-driven payments, and the emergence of agentic AI. Institutional adoption is rising, yet systemic risks, ethical concerns, and cybersecurity challenges persist. U.S. policy under the Trump administration is fostering a pro-crypto environment, with states adopting Bitcoin reserves. Meanwhile, the global rollout of CBDCs and tokenization of traditional assets is reshaping financial ecosystems. As tokenized products expand, balancing innovation with security and governance remains paramount.

Keywords: Tokenization; stablecoins; decentralized finance; agentic AI; central bank digital currencies; crypto payments & cybersecurity

With the approval of spot crypto ETFs in 2024 – bitcoin in January and ether in July – seemed to open the proverbial floodgates for crypto products and tokenization at large, these products merely represent the beginning of the tokenization process for financial markets at large. While crypto forwards and futures have been in existence for several years at this point, the totality of tokenization possibilities runs into the trillions of dollars, even if just surface level adoption occurs. For example, Blackrock, the world's largest asset manager and leading the bitcoin ETF space, has estimated the size of the tokenized asset marketplace to be $10 trillion. Given that it seems logical to conduct a deeper dive into a few of areas in which growth, adoption, and utilization continue to accelerate.

The approval of ETFs in the USA has also opened the proverbial door for any number of crypto-adjacent products and services in addition to the specific ETFs

Artificial Intelligence, ESG Investments and the Future of Tokenized Assets, 67–78

Published under exclusive licence by Emerald Publishing Limited
doi:10.1108/978-1-83708-108-020261008

linked to bitcoin and ether. For example, following the approval of these ETFs, the company Ripple (who had been battling with the SEC for years) achieved partial victory versus the SEC, has seen a dramatic recovery in the price of the XRP token, and has launched the RLUSD stablecoin, capitalizing on the double-digit growth of the stablecoin sector that saw the market capitalization exceed $200 billion during 2024.

Tokenization of financial markets can also raise the issues around the ethics and accessibility of this information to different classes of investors. Given the uproar that occurred as a result of the front-running that occurred during the GameStop trading frenzy during 2021–2022, revealing to mass market and retail traders that major TradFi institutions oftentimes obtain access to trading information, patterns, and records that are being conducted in real-time. For example, if tokenization does in fact increase the liquidity and trading options that are available to investors across the board, it stands to reason that the investors that will benefit the most from these developments will be the same investors that have already benefited from the massive investments in technology-driven trading algorithms (Wu et al., 2024).

In 2025, there was a slew of announcements connected to various cryptoassets seeking to launch ETFs or other tokenized products, with the expectation that due to the approval and success of both the bitcoin and ether ETFs that such a process would be simpler, cheaper, and easier.

DeFi

Decentralized finance, or DeFi, represents perhaps the single biggest change and evolution in the financial landscape since bitcoin burst into the mainstream conversation in 2017. In essence, what DeFi seeks to provide is many of the banking products and services without the need for centralized controls, products, or institutions. While seemingly an impossible task, decentralized protocols have already emerged into the mainstream marketplace as well as other decentralized autonomous organizations looking to raise capital, deploy solutions, and enact changes within the wider financial landscape (IMF, 2025). Let's take a look at a few of the core aspects of DeFi that have emerged as leading factors, as well as how AI can be used to improve DeFi processes. While the IRS has recently (end of 2024) instituted various tax data collection and reporting changes to make it simpler for agencies to collect data from DeFi providers, specifically the changes to IRS Code Section 6045 and 6050I, these remain options for individuals seeking to tap into potentially less liquid subsets of the crypto marketplace.

Decentralized finance is something that is virtually the complete opposite of the majority of TradFi institutions, payment processors, and other intermediaries that continue to dominate and play leading roles in U.S. financial markets. While it is worth noting that the majority of TradFi firms have implemented blockchain-based payment solutions and even tokenized payment offerings for customers/clients, these solutions are almost universally centralized in nature, reducing the effectiveness of the decentralized nature of these transactions. The implications of this growing competition – between truly decentralized platforms and payment options and centralized and centrally developed blockchain-based solutions – are set to redefine the conversations around tokenized services moving forward.

An additional aspect of DeFi that is just beginning to be discussed in wider policy circles is the overlap and functionality that can be created when tokenized payments and AI are integrated with each other. AI by its very nature and intended functionality is almost perfectly suited to leverage DeFi and decentralized payments versus other existing payment options.[1]

Staking

Crypto staking and staking-related operations are as aspect of tokenized financial markets that have been controversial for as long as the options have existed in the marketplace. To put it simply staking and the improvement to staking offerings has the real potential to open the door for greater investments from institutional and retail investors alike.

Crypto staking is the process of participating in a blockchain network by locking up cryptocurrency holdings to support its operations, such as validating transactions and securing the network. Staking is a fundamental component of Proof-of-Stake (PoS) and its variants (e.g., delegated PoS, liquid staking), which are consensus mechanisms designed as energy-efficient alternatives to Proof-of-Work (PoW). Participants, known as validators or delegators, commit their tokens to the network, and in return, they receive staking rewards – typically in the form of additional cryptocurrency. Validators are responsible for verifying transactions and adding new blocks to the blockchain.

The likelihood of being selected to validate a block often depends on the amount of crypto staked and the network's specific rules. Staking offers a way to earn passive income while contributing to blockchain security. However, risks include slashing penalties (losing staked assets due to malicious or negligent behavior), market volatility, and potential liquidity constraints since staked tokens may be locked for a period. With the rise of staking-as-a-service platforms and liquid staking derivatives, investors can stake without running their own validator nodes, increasing accessibility to the process.

Despite the seemingly well-understood technical components of staking and the importance of staking to the crypto ecosystem, there are still unresolved tax issues that continue to persist and cause issues for investors and users of staking-related services. These include, but are not limited to the following:

- *Taxable income*: Staking rewards are typically considered taxable when received. In the USA, for example, the IRS treats staking rewards as ordinary income, valued at the fair market price at the time of receipt. This means even if you don't sell, you owe taxes on the rewards.

[1]https://cointelegraph.com/news/how-to-legally-stake-crypto
https://www.chainalysis.com/blog/crypto-staking/
https://world.org/
https://www.businessinsider.com/worldcoin-sam-altman-iris-scanning-face-auth-tools-humanity-ubi-2024-8

- *Cost basis and capital gains*: When you later sell or trade your staking rewards, you could face capital gains tax. The taxable amount depends on the difference between the selling price and the fair market value when the rewards were received. Holding for more than a year may qualify for long-term capital gains tax rates, which are lower than short-term rates.
- *Slashing and losses*: If your staked assets are penalized (slashed) or their value drops, tax rules vary on whether these losses can be deducted.
- *Locked versus liquid staking*: Some tax authorities distinguish between rewards that are immediately available and those locked for a period, potentially affecting tax timing.
- *Reporting requirements*: Many countries require detailed reporting of staking income and sales, and failure to comply can lead to penalties.

Despite the arguments that continue to persist in the cryptoasset sector related to the tax treatment, the reality is that tax issues and treatment appear to have been well settled by the IRS. To that extent, it seems that while the issues facing this subset of the cryptoasset sector remain a long way from being resolved in a proactive manner, the rise of DeFi does provide a platform from which AI agents and bots can make payments and provide financing to a number of initiatives. As automation becomes more integrated within business operations, the need and desire for a payment option that can keep pace with the 24/7/365 up-time of AI will become an imperative.

AI-driven Payments and Services

Decentralized protocols have emerged as a viable option for lenders and companies seeking capital as traditional capital markets have experienced roadblocks and obstacles when seeking to provide capital to crypto organizations. For example, given the 24/7/365 up-time that is possible with the internet of things, AI-driven programs and applications, and the ability of tokenized payments to be conducted nearly instantaneously, it would seem to make sense that AI will take full advantage of crypto payments as the primary medium of exchange. The intersection of AI and crypto payments will only become more obvious are various real-world assets become tokenized and integrated within existing financial markets and structures (Xia et al., 2025). How this will play out on an individual basis will clearly differ depending on the organization in question but will also become more mainstream across economic areas regardless of which economic area or industry is being discussed.

AI bots will also play an important role as the Internet of Things economic begins to take shape and become more mainstream in nature, specifically as the adoption of AI by organizations for various roles continues to accelerate. As increasing amounts of business transactions make use of and leverage automation and AI, the question around how to appropriately compensate and pay for these services is also set to be a topic of growing importance. One other aspect that will need to be integrated within the controls and custody frameworks of all organizations is how the growing usage of tokenized assets might impact financial stability and risk management practices (FSB, 2024). Specifically, there is going to need to be a discussion related to developing payment and compensation solutions that mirror the instantaneous and 24/7/365 uptime availability of AI applications; blockchain and tokenized transactions seem to be a perfect fit.

AI and Stablecoins

Given the nearly continuous uptime that is possible via the continued growth and integration of AI throughout the marketplace, it would seem that the cross-over and intersection of AI and cryptoassets for transactional purposes would be inevitable. One such example of this integration and intersection would be the development of WorldCoin, which while not yet used as a medium of doing business in any major capacity has created significant buzz and excitement with regards to the future of these possibilities. Let's take a look at the specifics involved with WorldCoin, as well as the pros and cons of such a token, either now or in the future.

One of the most important aspects of WorldCoin is that it was founded by Sam Altman, who is the co-founder and CEO of OpenAI; the firm that has developed and launched ChatGPT, which in turn has created the first mass-market and widely understandable AI tool for even the novice user. Some of the core tenets that underpin the design and methodology for WorldCoin include, but are not limited to, the following:

- *Intersection of AI and crypto*: As might be expected, the primary underpinning of WorldCoin is the integration of AI to manage the creation, destruction, and management of the tokens themselves. The AI underpinning the WorldCoin protocol will automatically issue, trade, and monitor the issuance of tokens in a decentralized manner without the need for centrally planned or controlled protocols.
- *Connection to UBI*: One of the most common issues and fears that have accompanied the rise of AI into the mass market conversation is that the rise of AI will lead to mass job displacement and higher-than-ever unemployment. Setting aside the societal shifts and changes that will result from such large and sustained change in the employment rates and figures across the economy, there will also changes with regards to how firms need to operate.
    - o For example, if the employment levels across various socio-economic levels drop precipitously how will this change the consumption and purchasing patterns in the economy?
    - o If the total working population declines consistently over time, what will this do to other aspects of the economy such as education and housing?
- *Centralized paradox*: Even though the AI protocol itself will operate in decentralized manner in terms of token management, the reality is that WorldCoin is operated in a central manner. This is reinforced by the fact that in order to access and utilize WorldCoin tokens users must purchase and use a physical device known as an orb, in which these users must also hand over retinal information as well.

The intersection of AI, tokenized payments, and bio-metric data is perhaps the most interesting development of how AI and cryptoassets will continue to evolve and influence each other as the various marketplaces evolve over time. As these projects continue to evolve and develop from entry/pilot level stages to commercially viable projects, the implications of tokenized financial assets and markets will continue to be felt across the board (McKinsey & Company, 2024). WorldCoin, for all of the promise and potential that an AI-driven token might deliver, is also subject to multiple doubts, questions, and issues that will need to be addressed as the rise of both competitors (dollar-backed stablecoins) and AI-driven business processes will only increase moving forward.

Private Stablecoins

Stablecoins are arguably one of the most interesting subsets of the cryptoasset space, although the functionality of said cryptoassets is possibly the least exciting of the array of crypto products currently available. Put simply, stablecoins represent tokenized assets that are purpose built and developed to be used a medium of exchange versus cryptoassets such as bitcoin that although built as a decentralized cryptocurrency have not yet achieved widespread adoption as a medium of exchange. With a market capitalization of over $200 billion at the end of 2024/early 2025, following a year of dramatic growth and adoption that saw a double-digit growth, the private sector stablecoin marketplace has continued to experience growth, adoption, and better investor education.

Examples of stablecoins that have come to marketplace and that have achieved widespread adoption include, but are not limited, to USDT (issued by Tether), USDC (issued by Circle), and more recently PYUSD (issued by PayPal). Let's take a look at a few of the pros, cons, and adoption issues that have been connected to these stablecoins since launch and inception.

Tether and USDT: Tether has been the longest running stablecoin and has been circulated since 2013 and stands apart from other stablecoins in the marketplace in terms of both its longevity and the accounting, auditing, and reporting issues that have dogged the company for years. Following a legal settlement in 2019 with the New York Attorney General's office, and subsequent criticism and pressure to issue fully audited financial statements, the company took measures to improve these issues. Most importantly for market watchers, Tether has established a partnership with BDO Italia to improve the quality, consistency, and frequency of financial information.

Circle and USDC: Circle was launched following the dramatic run-up in bitcoin prices during 2017 and quickly established a reputation as a leading stablecoin focused on regulatory compliance and working within the establishing banking system. Before discussing other aspects of Circle, however, it is worth noting that despite these efforts USDC did suffer a significant depegging during the bank run and subsequent failure of SVB in March 2023. During the collapse, it was revealed that circle had over $3 billion in reserves at this banking institution, sending the price per coin briefly below $0.80 per token over that weekend.

With the news of a Circle IPO coming shortly, the rise of stablecoins continues virtually unabated even in the face of an increasingly competitive marketplace. Such a dramatic ascent in terms of market capitalization, utilization, and mass adoption comes with multiple implications for crypto investors and policy advocates alike. The issuers of USDC have filed an S-1 form with the SEC to list on the NYSE under symbol CRCL and reported $1.7 billion in reserve income from stablecoin operations at the end of 2024. Although USDC remains the second largest stablecoin when measured by market capitalization, approximately $60 billion compared to the over $140 billion of USDT (issued by Tether), the prospect of a Circle IPO has been generating market commentary and anticipation for years.

The most direct implication of this IPO is that the thawing of the previously ice and unhospitable environment for crypto firms under former SEC chairperson Gary Gensler is having real-world effects. In addition, the forthcoming Circle IPO, with primary advisor JP Morgan Chase, other crypto-native firms such as Ripple, Kraken, and Gemini have all indicated potential IPOs in the near future. While coming to market at a volatile time for the market as a whole, and specifically for technology stocks, the 36% growth in market capitalization of USDC – compared to 5% for USDT – has given investors cause for optimism.

The implications of the Circle IPO are set to be far-reaching throughout the marketplace but will also have an effect on the greater cryptoasset ecosystem, especially in light of policy changes that have been enacted under the second Trump administration in the USA.

With the return of Donald Trump to the White House in January 2025, the expectations and hope for the cryptoasset sector remain relatively high. For instance, following the inauguration and definitely expected within the first several months of the new administration, a bevy of executive orders and policy actions are expected that will directly affect the cryptoasset sector, including but not limited to the following.

1. Establishing a strategic bitcoin reserve
2. Establishing a federal-level digital asset stockpile comprised of non-bitcoin cryptoassets
3. Potentially modifying the tax code to minimize and/or eliminate all taxes currently applicable to crypto gains
4. Enacting legislative solutions and regulatory actions to attract investment and job creation connected to the cryptoasset sector to the USA
5. Making the USA the "crypto capital of the world"

Several of these actions have already been implemented via executive order, such as points #1 and #2 listed above, but more of the efforts that are widely anticipated changes to the broader environment are still very much works in progress. These include, but are not limited to, the efforts underway at the SEC to redress and reverse prior actions taken that were widely seen as stifling to innovation and growth of the crypto sector. In addition, the fact that despite statements to the contrary, that the potential for a U.S. CBDC still remains possible is an indication of the lack of consistency that policymakers have shown in drafting regulatory actions.

In addition to these efforts, there are also other efforts that have been launched at the state level, detailed below. Interestingly enough, the fact that individual states have taken the lead and have begun the process of developing bitcoin reserves and other pro-crypto laws is a reflection of both the decentralized nature of government as well as the interest that bitcoin and other crypto reserves have generated at the state level (WEF, 2025). Specifically, this course of action follows the lead that U.S. states have traditional taken in the creation of new industries and economic opportunities such as the credit card and insurance industries, which have taken hold in state.

As of early 2025, several U.S. states have introduced legislation to establish strategic Bitcoin reserves:

- *Texas*: In December 2024, Representative Giovanni Capriglione introduced a bill proposing the creation of a strategic Bitcoin reserve for the state. The legislation mandates that any Bitcoin acquired must remain in cold storage for at least five years, ensuring security and long-term value retention.
- *Pennsylvania*: In November 2024, Pennsylvania lawmakers proposed a bill that would enable the state to allocate up to 10% of its general, emergency, and state investment funds to Bitcoin. If enacted, this measure could lead to nearly $1 billion worth of Bitcoin being added to Pennsylvania's reserves, based on current valuations.
- *Ohio*: On December 17, 2024, Representative Derek Merrin introduced the Ohio Bitcoin Reserve Act, aiming to establish a Bitcoin fund within the state treasury. The act grants the Ohio treasurer discretion over the purchase and management of the asset.
- *New Hampshire*: On January 10, 2025, Representative Keith Ammon proposed a bill to allow the state's treasury to invest in Bitcoin. While Bitcoin is not mentioned by name in the bill, its market dominance makes it a likely candidate for inclusion.
- *North Dakota*: On January 10, 2025, North Dakota legislators introduced a resolution encouraging the state to invest a portion of its funds in digital assets and precious metals. While the resolution is less specific than formal legislation, it represents a step toward exploring Bitcoin's potential role in the state's treasury.
- *Wyoming*: On January 17, 2025, Wyoming introduced House Bill 201 to authorize state funds investment in Bitcoin, sponsored by Representatives Wasserburger, Brown, G, Filer, Lucas, and Singh, and Senator Smith, D.
- *Massachusetts*: On January 16, 2025, Massachusetts Senator Peter Durant introduced Senate Docket 422, titled "An Act Relative to a Bitcoin Strategic Reserve." The proposed bill would enable the Massachusetts State Treasurer to invest up to 10% of the annual deposits in the Commonwealth Stabilization Fund into Bitcoin or other digital assets.

By the end of Q1 2025, there were nearly 20 individual states that had created and progressed (to at least some extent) legislation and bills that would allow these states to invest certain portions of assets into bitcoin and other digital assets. The significance of this cannot be overstated as – until the present time – the investment of states and state affiliated agencies into bitcoin and other digital assets has the potential to redefine financial markets and the accounting for digital assets. The implications and significance of these government actors moving aggressively into bitcoin and other digital assets also have a potential downside effect; the lack of internal controls and control workflows at these entities can leave them as vulnerable targets for hackers.

The February 2025 hack of On February 21, 2025, Dubai-based cryptocurrency exchange Bybit experienced a significant security breach, resulting in the theft of approximately $1.5 billion worth of Ethereum (around 401,000 ETH). The incident occurred during a routine transfer from an offline "cold" wallet to a "warm" wallet used for daily operations. Hackers exploited this process, gaining control of the cold wallet and transferring its contents to an unknown address. Bybit's CEO, Ben Zhou, reassured users that the company remains solvent, with all client assets backed 1:1, and that withdrawals continue to be processed normally. The exchange is collaborating with blockchain forensic experts to trace the stolen funds and has offered a 10% bounty for assistance in recovering the assets. Blockchain analytics firms, including Elliptic, have attributed the attack to North Korea's Lazarus Group, known for previous large-scale cryptocurrency thefts. This event marks the largest cryptocurrency heist to date, surpassing previous records.[2]

Central Bank Digital Currencies

While private sector stablecoins have experienced dramatic and rapid growth since 2017–2018, these cryptoassets are not the only option that have emerged as a competition for bitcoin and other decentralized cryptocurrencies. As appealing and despite the high amounts of investment and interest that bitcoin has received the reality is that bitcoin and other decentralized tokens have not achieved mainstream adoption or utilization as a medium of exchange. This is the position that

---

[2]https://ag.ny.gov/press-release/2021/attorney-general-james-ends-virtual-currency-trading-platform-bitfinexs-illegal#:~:text=In%20the%20case%20of%20Tether,corners%20of%20the%20financial%20system.

https://www.wsj.com/articles/crypto-investors-cash-out-2-billion-in-usd-coin-after-bank-collapse 1338a80f?gaa_at=eafs&gaa_n=ASWzDAjWWvRGDxAsrxXwr6ubiQjAFPdwzN_d1sgjICgouAt0SaMSfQqU2r36Nfn5fVQ%3D&gaa_ts=68754563&gaa_sig=lC5w0oTyBrElB0eiO16Dp0sqAnEC_Fun3EDIbMUtMohWUsitKXe1uR8cllhv7iLKJAKNU76QsOLyI2U6xT4vOw%3D%3D

https://www.wilsoncenter.org/article/bybit-heist-what-happened-what-now#:~:text=On%20February%2021%2C%202025%20North,security%20in%20the%20crypto%20industry stablecoins were originally designed to fulfill and meet, but governments and other established centers of power remain unlikely to sit back and let the private sector fulfill the needs of currency from both individuals and institutions.

Currency has long been one of the most levers via which governments and other centrally organized seats of power have exercised control over businesses, individuals, and international trade. Even with the rapid growth of stablecoins, the overall market capitalization remains a very small percentage of global currency markets. Specifically, the stablecoin market size breached $200 billion at the end of 2024 versus the total FX market that is measured in trillions. Given the benefits delivered by tokenized transactions – speed, traceability, and transparency – have not gone unnoticed by governments. If, the thinking has gone, governments and central banks could capture the benefits and upsides of tokenized transactions, it could improve the processing of payments both on a national and international basis. This is also why, despite public comments and statements deriding bitcoin and other decentralized cryptocurrencies as purely speculative plays and investment options, virtually every major TradFi institutions (including banks) have implemented blockchain-based payment options.

One additional change that has evolved as a result of the greater realization of the benefits of tokenization is the governments across the world have begun to experiment, test, and deploy cryptoassets known as central bank digital currencies. In essence, these tokens are seeking to merge the benefits of fiat currencies – wide acceptance and relatively stable valuation – with the speed and efficiency delivered by tokenized payments. The development of these CBDCs has been stalled by legitimate concerns around privacy, the possibility of surveillance, and the possible development of a surveillance state.

Despite the justifiable pushback against the rise of a centrally controlled and managed crypto-token, it remains virtually assured that existing fiat currencies will embrace some components of tokenization over time. This makes sense for any number of reasons, but primarily because the governments in question want to capture the upsides of tokenized payments without losing control over the currency markets.[3]

Where Tokenization Moves Next

Following the approval of spot crypto ETFs in 2024, there was an anticipation and expectation that more tokenized products and services would come to market in relatively short order, but the pace of adoption and implementation has been much slower. This has to do with a number of factors, including but not limited to governmental hesitation, fears related to speculation, and price volatility that

---

[3]https://www.skadden.com/insights/publications/2022/02/the-federal-reserve-weighs-risks#:~:text=Changes%20to%20financial%2Dsector%20market,that%20a%20user%20could%20hold
https://www.dhs.gov/sites/default/files/2024-09/2024aepphaselllcombattingillicitactivityutilizingfinancial.pdf

are justifiable given the volatile nature of bitcoin and other cryptocurrencies, as well as the regulatory regimes across the world had not always been perceived as pro-crypto. The outcome of the 2024 U.S. Presidential election has shifted the narrative significantly in the USA, with the first pro-crypto Congress having been sworn in, and a President in Donald Trump that has publicly stated his support and appeal.

One of the most significant opportunities for expanded tokenization options is that traditional financial assets and data will be put on-chain and tokenized over time. While the main conversations around this topic have focused on the financial implications of these efforts, there is also the possibility that wider swaths of information will become tokenized over time. Specifically, subsets of information connected to real estate, healthcare data, educational records, and employment records all have the likelihood of becoming tokenized, put on-chain, and accessible in an on-demand methodology. While this has the potential to make accessing data more efficient and available on a real-time basis, it also potentially exposes the data to hacking attempts and other cybersecurity issues.

Using cryptoassets for payments can bring speed and innovation, but it also opens the door to new cybersecurity risks. Unlike traditional payment systems, which are tightly regulated and centrally managed, crypto transactions often happen on decentralized networks. Even bitcoin, which has been adopted as the crypto of choice for institutional players, still runs on top of a globally decentralized network. This can make them harder to trace, harder to reverse, and more appealing to hackers.

One major risk comes from user error. If someone clicks on a phishing link or accidentally shares their private wallet key, there's often no way to get that money back. There is no customer service line to call – once it's gone, it's gone. Many investors still do not fully understand how to keep their digital assets secure, and that creates an opportunity for bad actors. This also reinforces the helps explain the surge in demand that followed the approval of spot crypto ETFs such as bitcoin and ether; combining the upside and traceability of on-chain assets with the security and custody provided b.

Then, there's the technology itself. Many newer crypto platforms and tokens are launched quickly, sometimes without thorough security testing. Bugs in smart contracts – pieces of code that automatically handle transactions – can be exploited to steal funds or break the system. There have already been large-scale hacks that have drained millions from exchanges and crypto apps, and even as crypto becomes more mainstream, the pace of hacks and breaches has only accelerated. As more payment systems connect to different blockchains across borders, the complexity increases – and so do the security challenges. Add to that a lack of clear regulations, and it becomes even harder to track and prevent fraud or theft.

In short, crypto payments can be powerful, but they are not risk-free due to both price volatility and the exposure that can result as tokenized transactions and options are integrated alongside TradFi payment rails. As adoption grows, the industry will need to double down on security education, smart design, and better protections to keep users safe.

The chapter examines the accelerating integration of tokenization into global financial markets, driven by the approval of spot Bitcoin and Ether ETFs in 2024. The chapter highlights key developments including stablecoins, DeFi, staking, AI-driven payments, and CBDCs, emphasizing their transformative potential. Institutional adoption is rising, particularly amid a pro-crypto U.S. policy environment, yet tokenized markets introduce systemic risks, tax complexity, and cybersecurity concerns. The convergence of AI and blockchain is creating new opportunities – especially in automation and payments – while also raising ethical, governance, and security questions. Ultimately, balancing innovation, financial inclusion, and regulatory oversight is essential to realizing tokenization's long-term potential.

References

FSB. (2024). *The financial stability implications of tokenisation*. Financial Stability Board Report.

IMF. (2025). Tokenization and financial market inefficiencies. *IMF Economic Review*, *63*(1).

McKinsey & Company. (2024). Tokenized financial assets: From pilot to scale. *McKinsey Insights*.

WEF Asset Tokenization. (2025). *Asset tokenization in financial markets: The next generation of innovation*. World Economic Forum Report.

Wu, H., Yao, Q., Liu, Z., Huang, B., Zhuang, Y., Tang, H., & Liu, E. (2024). *Blockchain for finance: A survey*. arXiv. https://doi.org/10.48550/arXiv.2402.17219

Xia, N., Zhao, X., Yang, Y., Li, Y., & Li, Y. (2025). *Exploration on real-world assets and tokenization*. arXiv. https://doi.org/10.48550/arXiv.2503.01111

Chapter 9

Accounting Services in a Tokenized World

Abstract

The approval of spot Bitcoin and Ether ETFs in 2024 has ignited widespread interest in tokenization, with market potential estimated at $10 trillion. This shift is accelerating the adoption of decentralized finance (DeFi), crypto staking, artificial intelligence (AI)-driven payments, and private stablecoins. Innovations such as agentic AI and blockchain integration are transforming financial services, though they introduce systemic risks and cybersecurity challenges. U.S. federal and state policies are increasingly supportive of digital assets, including state-level Bitcoin reserves. Meanwhile, the global rise of CBDCs reflects governments' intent to harness tokenization's benefits while maintaining monetary control. Ensuring security, transparency, and governance remains critical.

Keywords: Tokenization; stablecoins; crypto accounting; crypto auditing; central bank digital currencies; crypto cybersecurity

One of the most important changes and modifications that will come to pass as tokenization and blockchain-based assets become more mainstream is how the accounting and attestation landscape will evolve going forward (Singh, 2025). Returning back to the fundamentals of blockchain technology, enabling transparent, traceable, and real-time transactions and access to information, there are several distinct effects that this technology will have on accounting and financial services.

1. More real-time information and reporting. One of the most obvious implications of tokenized information is that there is going to be greater availability of real-time data to all internal and external stakeholders. This will take the form of both qualitative and quantitative information, all of which

Artificial Intelligence, ESG Investments and the Future of Tokenized Assets, 79–86

Published under exclusive licence by Emerald Publishing Limited
doi:10.1108/978-1-83708-108-020261009

is increasingly expected to be analyzed and reported to investors, regulators, and other stakeholder groups. Given that the traditional audit, accounting, and tax reporting practices have encountered significant time delays, the implications of real-time availability of data will allow more real-time financial reporting.

2. Increased focus on data quality and accuracy. Combined with the first point related to the availability of real-time financial markets data, there will also be an increased focus on accurate and relevant data. Especially in the age of social media, external users that require analytics and reporting on virtually every subset of data produced by an organization means that the tolerance for errors will decline as well. With AI allowing errors and data abnormalities to be contained and dealt with as they occur, as well as blockchain creating an immutable record of data, investors and other users of financial statement data will have a much lower tolerance for restatements and other financial corrections.
3. More pressure on accounting and auditing standard setters. While it seems natural to expect lower rates of errors as automation, AI, and blockchain become more integrated within financial services, the reality is that the audit profession is in the midst of a crisis. No matter which metric is used, including the PCAOB data referenced previously in this text, the fact remains that the audit field is in the midst of a reputational and logistical slide. Investors increasingly see the issues with backward-looking and long-delayed audit reports, non-CPAs firms continue to make inroad into the audit and attestation fields, and the regulatory importance of said services continues to be questioned. Whether it is via increased AI utilization or broader use of on-chain assets, the expectations for more real-time and on-demand audit data are set to only increase.

Accounting for Tokenized Assets

The accounting for tokenized assets is conversation that has continued to evolve and develop over time, especially with the issuance and approval of ASC 2023-08, but with the continued evolution of tokenized assets, there will be emerging questions and topics that need to be addressed as the ecosystem evolves (Silva & Costa, 2024). Let's take a look at a few of the items and considerations that CPAs for tokenized assets will need to change.

The rapid evolution of DeFi is presenting new challenges and opportunities for accounting professionals. As DeFi continues to disrupt traditional financial systems, key trends are emerging in accounting and financial reporting:

- *Regulatory uncertainty and emerging standards*
  Regulators worldwide are working to establish guidelines for DeFi transactions, which are often executed via smart contracts without intermediaries. The Financial Accounting Standards Board (FASB) and International Financial Reporting Standards have started addressing the classification, measurement,

and disclosure of digital assets, though DeFi-specific standards remain underdeveloped. As regulations become clearer, accountants must stay updated on evolving compliance obligations.

- *Fair value accounting for cryptoassets*
  Traditional accounting practices have struggled with DeFi-related assets due to high volatility and liquidity variations. The recent move toward fair value accounting for cryptocurrencies under FASB guidelines is a step forward in providing more transparent and relevant financial reporting for DeFi assets.
- *Auditing challenges in DeFi transactions*
  DeFi protocols operate on public blockchains, making transactions highly transparent but also complex to verify. Accountants and auditors are increasingly relying on blockchain analytics tools to track DeFi activities, including liquidity pools, staking rewards, and governance token transactions. The challenge remains in verifying smart contract risks and ensuring financial accuracy without centralized oversight.
- *Tax compliance and reporting innovations*
  DeFi taxation is a growing concern, as jurisdictions require detailed transaction records for activities such as yield farming, staking, and lending. Tax authorities, including the IRS, are strengthening DeFi reporting requirements. Accountants are leveraging AI-powered tax automation tools to ensure compliance.
- *AI and automation in DeFi accounting*
  AI-driven accounting solutions are emerging to handle real-time reconciliation, fraud detection, and risk assessment for DeFi transactions. These tools help accountants manage the complexity of DeFi financial reporting, reducing manual errors and improving audit readiness.

As DeFi adoption grows, accountants must integrate blockchain expertise, regulatory knowledge, and advanced technology to ensure transparency, compliance, and financial accuracy.

How Tokenization Will Impact Auditing and Attestation Services

The tokenization of financial services is already set to drive innovation, disruption, and change throughout the entire financial services sector and space, but one area in particular seems almost tailor-made to be upended as tokenization occurs throughout almost every aspect of the economic landscape; auditing and attestation of financial information. To fully encapsulate this discussion, let's examine the current issues with the audit and attestation field, as well as how tokenization will alter these items.

Current Issues with Auditing and Attestation

Some of the most significant issues that currently exist within the audit and attestation subfields are the following two realities. First, not all data that is subjected to audits and other attestation efforts is standardized, easily divisible nor is the totality of data subject to audits on a periodic basis. This is also why the number of audit failures, frauds, and substantial audit issues continues to rise and generate headlines even as the importance of auditing and reporting information to the stakeholder community. Second, the tokenization of financial services will sub-divide the trading and holding of various financial instruments, even TradFi instruments such as equity and debt instruments. In essence, the tokenization of financial assets also has the potential to increase the volatility associated and linked with these financial instruments due to the wider marketplace that now has access to the instruments.

Tokenization also has the potential to offset and potentially degrade the effectiveness of internal controls that institutions have currently put in place around financial assets and information. With greater levels of liquidity, the placement of assets and other information on-chain and the wider availability of trading and liquidity can lead to controls and safeguards developed for a trading environment constrained by the guardrails of TradFi markets and regulators.

Tokenization-related Issues for Auditing and Internal Controls

One major risk is loss of centralized oversight, as blockchain transactions often operate on decentralized networks, reducing the ability of organizations to enforce traditional controls. This decentralization can make it harder to detect unauthorized transactions, increasing the risk of fraud or misappropriation of assets.

Additionally, immutability of blockchain records means that errors or fraudulent transactions cannot be easily reversed, creating difficulties in error correction and financial reporting. Access control issues may also arise, as digital assets require strong cryptographic protections. If private keys are lost or stolen, the associated assets may be irrecoverable, leading to significant financial losses.

Furthermore, valuation and audit complexities can undermine financial reporting accuracy. Tokenized assets may be subject to volatile market pricing, and their valuation can be challenging due to the lack of standardized accounting guidelines. Auditors may struggle to verify ownership and transaction authenticity, increasing compliance risks.

Finally, regulatory uncertainty surrounding asset tokenization can lead to inconsistent reporting and governance practices, further weakening internal control frameworks and exposing firms to legal risks. Organizations must adapt internal controls to mitigate these challenges effectively. The debate around internal controls and the effect of controls on the operating environment of these firms is an ongoing conversation.

The 2025 efforts by the U.S. Congress to undo reporting obligations for decentralized trading and reporting operations underline the policy pivot that has occurred since the most recent U.S. Presidential election. On April 10, 2025, President Donald Trump signed a bill that officially repealed the IRS's controversial "DeFi Broker Rule." Originally finalized in late 2024 under the Biden administration, the rule would have required DeFi platforms to report user transactions to the IRS using Form 1099-DA, starting in 2027.

The rule was meant to bring more transparency to crypto transactions, but it quickly drew criticism from both sides of the aisle. Lawmakers, including Senator Ted Cruz (R-TX) and Representative Mike Carey (R-OH), led the charge to overturn it using the Congressional Review Act. They argued that DeFi platforms simply don't have the same structure or access to user data that traditional brokers do. Asking them to comply with standard tax reporting, they said, was unrealistic and could drive innovation overseas.

Supporters of the repeal emphasized that DeFi's decentralized nature makes this kind of compliance technically impossible in many cases. They warned that overregulation could stunt the growth of the U.S. crypto industry.

However, not everyone celebrated the repeal. Opponents cautioned that removing these rules could open the door to tax evasion, money laundering, and other illicit activity. According to the Congressional Budget Office, the repeal could add $4.5 billion to the federal deficit by 2035.

Even with the rule gone, crypto investors are still responsible for reporting their gains and losses. The IRS still has tools like audits and summonses to enforce compliance – and under the CRA, similar rules can't be reintroduced without new legislation.

AI-driven Financial Services

One of the most significant changes and innovations that are able to be created via the integration of AI throughout financial services is real-time trading and reporting insights that will be able to be customized, reported, and analyzed by market actors across both the public sector and private sector. As these AI and automation-driven applications continue to permeate the business landscape, these factors are also being covered and taught in business schools as well as continuing education within the profession (Mulyadi & Anwar, 2025). While automated trading, primarily driven by bots or other algorithmic actors, has been in existence for decades at this point, the advent and implementation of more sophisticated AI and GenAI protocols will allow even more significant insights, dashboards, and reports to be customized and delivered on a continuous basis, which has been. While the majority of the focus has pertained to the implications for the private sector, it is also worth noting that the public sector will also benefit and embrace these technologies.

One of the largest and most significant benefits that will be delivered to the public sector is that as blockchain-based transactions and data become more mainstream and available on an everyday basis is that governments and other governmental agencies will have real-time access to tax, employment, and other data used during the normal course of business. Especially since the data stored and verified on an underlying blockchain is, in fact, verified by the members of that blockchain, this enables AI-driven processes to be accomplished in more trustworthy manner. This combination and integration between blockchain and AI represents a substantial advancement in how financial data can be collected, analyzed, and reported.

The effect of this real-time analytics and reporting possibilities will have ramifications for both the private sector firms implementing these real-time reporting systems, as well as the regulators, tax authorities, and governmental agencies tasked with analyzing these reports and information. For example, tax authorities will have complete and real-time access to all applicable transactions and payments that will be part of the tax assessment process. Securities regulators, including the SEC as well as international counterparts, will have access to financial information, records, and financial statements as they are being assembled as opposed to having to wait weeks (or even months) to gain access to these data.

Employment implications of greater AI integration are going to be significant, especially for individuals and analysts that have spent large amounts of time analyzing, reviewing, and reporting out to the marketplace. For these individuals, who will most likely be lower level or newer hired employees, education around the specifics of AI as well as the effect of AI on implementation current jobs, future employment opportunities, and how the company will evolve going forward (NJCPA, 2025). These educational efforts are important not only from an informational perspective but also as to how it will effectively drive...

One aspect and other item that will need to be incorporated as AI becomes more widespread and integrated within financial services is the simple fact that AI has the ability to make decisions, grant credit, allocate capital, and otherwise evaluate business decisions, clients, and otherwise interact with both the grantors and recipients of capital. Linking back to the earlier conversation in this text, the ability of AI to actively allocate capital, make personnel decisions, and otherwise directly impact the business decision-making process will need to develop new and emerging financial service opportunities. Specifically, the ability of AI to complement and augment the rise of decentralized financial services is set to play an integral role in the DeFi sector.

Decentralized and Autonomous Financial Futures

Before speaking more in-depth about the potential for DeFi and the impact of AI on the decentralized financial landscape, it is worth conducting a drilldown on one of the most important innovations in the blockchain and tokenized space; decentralized autonomous organizations (DAOs). Interestingly enough, the rise of the DAO has also seen a parallel rise in another important blockchain application, smart contracts, which will be examined in more depth below. Let's take a look at a few of the core characteristics that set DAOs apart from both other blockchain-based organizations and other AI-driven organizations that have existed in the marketplace.

Smart contracts: One of the most important aspects and tools, as discussed previously within this book, is the rise and continued implementation of smart contracts in the tokenized asset ecosystem. Smart contacts, despite the name and connotations associated therein, are neither smart nor are they universally perceived to be contracts in the classical sense. Instead, these blockchain applications represent programmable code that is embedded into an underlying blockchain that allows the automation or at least partial automation of certain business processes. In order to have an organization operate in a truly decentralized manner, however, the various blockchains and tokenized instruments must be able to coordinate and collaborate across different blockchains and asset networks.

Decentralized governance: As the name might suggest the governance and operations of a DAO area decentralized in nature, this involves decentralizing the governance of how some organizations and businesses operate. In terms of actually attempting to decentralized corporate governance, which by its default nature is usually managed and controlled by the organization in question. How this usually plays out is the organization in question hires some independent contractors and individuals to serve as a.

One of the core aspects and greatest promises of the combination of AI and tokenization is that financial services, products, and activities will continue to operate on a global and eventually decentralized basis. Specifically, the ability of tokenized payments, via blockchain technology and blockchain-adjacent tools and services, will enable real-time transmission and confirmation of data between various counterparties as it pertains to banking, payments, and the settlement of payments between various entities. This relatively simple change and innovation will radically reshape the current banking system as well as the role of financial intermediaries in the banking process. In addition to the disruption that such a change will cause, it will also create opportunities for proactive and forward looking financial professionals and firms seeking to leverage the advances in automation to drive changes both internally and externally facing.

DAOs are also already present in the marketplace, despite the continuing legal and economic challenges that can make further development and implementation difficult from a legal, organizational, and accounting perspective. Let's take a look at a few of the highest profile DAOs that have been emerged and interacted with the broader marketplace since the concept first achieved mainstream awareness and engagement.

ConstitutionDAO and CityDAO are examples of DAOs that showcase innovative uses of blockchain technology to enable collective action and governance.

ConstitutionDAO was a short-lived, community-driven project launched in 2021 to purchase one of the 13 surviving original copies of the U.S. Constitution at a Sotheby's auction. Through crowdfunding via Ethereum, the DAO raised over $47 million from thousands of contributors globally. ConstitutionDAO demonstrated the power of blockchain to organize decentralized communities rapidly. Despite their bid being unsuccessful, the project highlighted both the potential and challenges of DAOs, such as governance complexity and fund redistribution.

CityDAO is an ongoing initiative focused on experimenting with decentralized land ownership and governance. Inspired by the concept of smart cities,

CityDAO acquired a parcel of land in Wyoming, leveraging the state's progressive DAO legislation. Members, known as "citizens," can participate in decision making and governance, exploring ideas like tokenized land ownership, decentralized infrastructure, and collaborative urban planning. CityDAO serves as a testbed for using blockchain to reimagine how communities manage land and resources collaboratively.

Both projects underscore the promise of DAOs for enabling novel, community-led initiatives but also highlight the challenges of coordination, scalability, and regulatory navigation in the evolving landscape of decentralized governance.

Decentralization is almost the complete opposite of how current financial markets, products, and services currently operate, with a singular point of control, focus, and custody over financial information. This current system of centrally controlled and monitored data is a direct result of the fact that until recently the technology simply did not exist to enable decentralized and/or distributed models of management and operations to successfully take place. Thanks to advances in automation and AI, however, the processing and computing power is finally available to allow real-time analytics, data gathering, and reporting of these insights out to the marketplace on an on-demand basis.

One additional factor should be kept in mind as well; with automation, real-time analytics, and data that is already confirmed by the members of the blockchain network itself, a reasonable question to ask is whether or not the accounting and auditing function will be as necessary going forward as it had been in the past. Especially given the rise of non-certified individuals and firms seeking to offer services connected to financial reporting, the risk of decentralization further undermining the need for certified professionals will only increase.

This chapter analyzes how tokenization, blockchain, and AI reshape accounting, auditing, and assurance. Continuous on-chain data streams enable near-real-time financial reporting, intensify demands for data quality, and pressure standard setters to update recognition and disclosure frameworks, particularly for DeFi, staking, and stablecoin activities. Fair-value measurement, smart-contract verification, and blockchain analytics tools emerge as critical competencies for CPAs. Audit risk shifts from sampling to continuous monitoring, while decentralized architectures challenge internal controls and custody frameworks. Regulatory reversals, such as repeal of the DeFi broker rule, underscore policy volatility. Ultimately, governance, cybersecurity, and AI oversight become prerequisites for trustworthy tokenized financial reporting.

References

Mulyadi, M., & Anwar, Y. (2025). Business school teaching case study: taking accountancy from spreadsheets to AI. *Financial Times Case Studies*.

Silva, J., & Costa, M. (2024). The future of accounting: How will digital transformation impact the sector? *Journal of Digital Accounting*.

Singh, A. (2025). The future of accounting: How AI and automation are changing the profession. *International Journal for Multidisciplinary Research*, *7*(2).

Chapter 10

Emerging Technologies and Future Financial Services

Abstract

This chapter explores how emerging technologies – especially AI, blockchain, and stablecoins – are transforming the accounting and financial services landscape. It outlines the implications for Certified Public Accountant (CPA) workforce trends, real-time data demands, advisory services, and margin compression. It also analyzes recent U.S. policy shifts under the Trump administration, including the GENIUS Act and pro-crypto regulatory changes at the SEC and OCC, as catalysts for digital dollar dominance. Additional focus is placed on AI regulation, ESG-driven power needs, and the evolving role of financial professionals. Ultimately, the chapter argues that strategic adaptation and continuous upskilling are essential for navigating this rapidly digitizing environment.

Keywords: Accounting; digital asset policy; CPA workforce; blockchain; emerging technologies

The implications of the emerging technologies discussed and presented within this book are significant, will be widespread, and will also have ramifications throughout virtually every aspect of the financial sector. Let's take a look at a few of them below.

CPA pipeline: The CPA pipeline is perhaps one of the most complicated and multifaceted challenges facing that accounting and audit profession. What this means, in other words, is that the issues that have created the shortage of newer entrants to the profession will not be able to be addressed or solved with one solution or idea. Rather this is a problem that took decades to create and will take nearly as long to solve. Emerging technologies, however, have an important role to play in doing just that. Specifically, the increased investment in automation and

Artificial Intelligence, ESG Investments and the Future of Tokenized Assets, 87–102

Published under exclusive licence by Emerald Publishing Limited
doi:10.1108/978-1-83708-108-020261010

technologies such as AI are already sending changes throughout the profession, with fears of job automation and obsolescence becoming widespread in certain accounting circles. That said, the reality is that while some jobs and tasks will become more automated over time will become an increasingly self-evident aspect of the financial services job market and industry.

The implications of greater automation and AI integration within the accounting and CPA profession are several and need to be understood both in terms of the impact they will have on specific jobs and practice management. While automation might initially take jobs and tasks at the lower level or entry level tiers of the organization, this will not remain the reality forever. As automation continues to accelerate, both inside firms and outside via client adoption, the need for partners to develop and bring in business will also be reduced. For example, as automation takes more work and therefore billable hours, how easy will it be for partners to build out lucrative books of business in emerging fields? Compounding this factor, how easy will it be to convince potential clients to pay the rates necessary to support multiple partners in emerging areas. Consider the following scenario: as automation frees up time and employee hours, this will lead to less time needed to complete the tasks this fact will not go unnoticed by potential clients.

Demand for real-time data and reports: One of the most consistent issues and complaints that users of financial information have with the producers and communicators of said data is that the information is often times out of date. Be it in the form of financial statements, audited financial reports, or even tax planning and payment information, the reality is that financial services is almost always a backward looking endeavor. This is set to change with the increased automation – be it AI driven or otherwise, but it also something that institutions are going to need to plan for as well as the deluge of information that is produced by organizations in virtually every industry.

Especially as the influence of tokenization (which will enable deeper and more liquid trading) as well as AI looks set to accelerate the pace of transactions and data production, the need for updated and improved auditing and reporting practices will need to evolve as well. While proof-of-reserves and proof-of-solvency look positioned to the effectuate the necessary change in order for accounting professionals to audit and provide attestation services for blockchain services, there remains substantial work to be done in other areas of the review and attestation fields.

Future Role for Financial Professionals

As finance, accounting, and technology increasingly become overlapping areas of expertise and information it is reasonable the role and purpose of financial services professionals will also need to update the collective skill sets and data sets that are used to provide advisory and other business services to external clients. Given the growing acceleration of technological integration and adoption across the board the future of accounting and financial services is set to evolve in a number of different directions.

Pivot to advisor: At virtually every level and across the wider accounting and financial landscape, the desire for accounting professionals to be treated as a business partner and strategic advisor versus a compliance focused professional. Alongside this desire to alter perception, there is also a growing shift – discussed throughout this text – toward the demand and expectation for information of all kinds to be prepared, reported, and ready for analytics in a real-time manner.

Margin compression: As with any other recently adapted technology the primary and initial effect of more automation and technology, there will be an impact related to the prices that customers and clients are willing to pay for these services. Following similar patterns that have emerged in TradFi institutions, with greater automation and real-time analytics leading to lower margins – and in many cases – an elimination of margins altogether. The compression and potential elimination of margins in the accounting industry have the potential to further exacerbate the pipeline issues that are already facing the profession due to competition from non-accounting professionals and other technologically oriented firms. Measures to address this margin compression include the pivot to value pricing, modifying work-from-office or work-from-home policies, and other ways in which firms seek to attract and retain talent.

Higher standards and expectations: Alongside the need and expectations of customers and clients for more on-demand information and analytics there will also be a growing expectation among clients for higher standards, more transparency, and more real-time insights. This also will have the effect of bringing higher levels of scrutiny to the auditing and accounting professionals, following the higher failure rates that had been identified by the PCAOB. With the number of hacks, breaches, and other data incidents that occur time and time again in the USA and other marketplaces, when combined with the ever-increasing amount of personal and institutional data becoming digitized, stored, and transferred in a digital manner, there will be a growing amount of pressure to store and manage these information streams going forward.

Non-CPA competition: The competition for accounting and accounting-adjacent services has already accelerated the rise of non-CPA firms performing services for external clients. While in most cases, this does not result in any significant damage to either the firm or clients involved, the possibility of these new entrants to the field also create an opportunity alongside the more obvious competitive implications. It is true that more competition for existing services and practices, referenced in the margin compression note documented previously, will indeed occur, but it will also open the door to new services lines and opportunities.

In recent developments within the accounting industry, some CPAs employed by private equity (PE)-owned firms are being instructed to remove the "CPA" designation from their email signatures and even from professional profiles like LinkedIn. This directive stems from the adoption of alternative practice structures (APS) by these firms, wherein audit and assurance services are provided by a CPA-owned entity, while advisory and other services are delivered by a separate, non-CPA firm under the same brand. The rationale is to prevent public confusion regarding the firm's licensing status.

Specifically as clients and customers become more comfortable and experienced with the fields of tokenized payments, there will be the opportunity for CPAs to (1) understand how these technologies work and operate in the marketplace and (2) build out services that complement the existing service opportunities already performed by CPAs. This is already occurring, with most of the largest 20–25 firms in the USA developing and marketing service lines adjacent to the emerging technology fields.

At this point, it is also worth documenting and discussing how policy changes in the USA are driving innovation and change in the areas of emerging technologies and the new areas in which they are creating new opportunities for financial professionals seeking to implement these tools going forward. While the USA is one singular marketplace, it is also the marketplace that has the deepest and most liquid financial marketplace in the world, and changes that occur in this market will have ripple effects across the globe.

Policy Changes in the USA

Following the re-election of Donald Trump and the bevy of executive orders that were signed during the first few weeks in office the policy and policy outlook in the USA for cryptoassets. In addition to the executive order that has been issued, the Trump administration has appointed pro-crypto individuals to head up various federal agencies as well as supporting efforts to reverse and repeal certain tax policies that had been pursued under previous administrations. Highlighting this fact is the inaugural White House Summit on Digital Assets, drawing industry leaders, CEOs, investors, and policy advocates to discuss how policy developments can support U.S. crypto investments and innovation moving forward.

Included in the executive order that was issued by the White House several important points were specified, which include but are not limited to, the following.

On January 23, 2025, President Donald Trump signed Executive Order 14178, titled "Strengthening American Leadership in Digital Financial Technology." This directive aims to bolster the USA' position in the digital asset sector by promoting innovation, ensuring regulatory clarity, and safeguarding economic freedom.

Key provisions:

1. *Establishment of the presidential working group on digital asset markets*: This group, chaired by the Special Advisor for AI and Crypto, includes high-ranking officials such as the Secretary of the Treasury and the Chairman of the Securities and Exchange Commission. Its mandate is to develop a federal regulatory framework for digital assets, including stablecoins, and to assess the feasibility of creating a national digital asset stockpile, potentially utilizing cryptocurrencies seized by federal law enforcement.
2. *Revocation of previous directives*: The order rescinds Executive Order 14067 of March 9, 2022, titled "Ensuring Responsible Development of Digital Assets," and the Department of the Treasury's "Framework for International Engagement on Digital Assets" issued on July 7, 2022. Consequently,

all related policies and guidance are nullified to realign with the new administration's objectives.

3. *Prohibition of Central Bank Digital Currencies (CBDCs)*: The executive order explicitly bans the establishment, issuance, or promotion of CBDCs within the USA and abroad, citing concerns over financial stability, individual privacy, and national sovereignty. It mandates the immediate termination of any ongoing federal initiatives related to CBDCs.
4. *Promotion of open blockchain networks*: The order emphasizes the protection and promotion of individuals' and private entities' rights to access and utilize open public blockchain networks for lawful purposes. This includes the development and deployment of software, participation in mining activities, and conducting transactions without unlawful censorship.
5. *Advancement of dollar-backed stablecoins*: To reinforce the sovereignty of the U.S. dollar, the order advocates for the development and global promotion of lawful dollar-backed stablecoins, viewing them as complementary to traditional banking and financial systems.

An additional and interesting quirk of U.S. crypto policy under the 2nd Trump Administration is that while the launch of a CBDC has been officially banned, that private sector stablecoins are going to be prioritized by the USA going forward. How this could play out will differ depending on which cryptoassets are prioritized, but there are several key points and factors that are going to play dominant roles and factors in the U.S. financial markets that need to increasingly compete with other currencies for leadership positions in the global marketplace.

By fostering the growth of stablecoins, the administration aims to increase global demand for the U.S. dollar, as these digital assets require reserves in U.S. currency. This strategy is expected to bolster the dollar's position as the world's primary reserve currency and medium of exchange.

Stablecoins look set to support the continuing strength of the U.S. dollar going forward, even in the face of growing international competition. While past efforts to supplant the U.S. dollar as the global reserve currency have occurred, the strength of this competition has continued to increase over the coming decades. Be it the government of mainland China, the European Union, or the possibility of a BRIC currency coming back to the proverbial table.

However, this approach has drawn criticism from some financial experts. Hedge fund Elliott Management, for instance, has warned that the administration's support for cryptocurrencies could be fueling a speculative bubble, potentially leading to significant market disruptions if it bursts.

In summary, the Trump administration's endorsement of dollar-backed stablecoins, coupled with its rejection of a CBDC, reflects a strategic effort to maintain and strengthen the U.S. dollar's supremacy in the evolving digital financial landscape.

Stablecoins seem set to continue to dominate the cryptoasset landscape in terms of utilization of cryptoassets as a medium of exchange versus simply using these tokens as investment options. The fact that the U.S. government is now actively encouraging the utilization of these options for dollar support purposes indicates the understanding that stablecoins are a strategic tool for policymakers and institutions alike. As the dollar faces continued and increasing competition from currencies such as the Chinese yuan, the newly issued and created BRIC common currency, and even the Euro that had served as an ally to the USA in previous trade wars and currency competitions now engaged in a number of trade spats against the USA illustrates the growing competition and potential threats to U.S. dollar leadership.

The prioritization of stablecoins and crypto payments in the USA has been an ongoing issue and project that multiple lawmakers have prioritized during the last few years and especially during the post-FTX collapse. With the U.S. federal policy priorities shifting and highlighting the importance of clearer and more consistent regulations at the federal level, the reality is that crypto standards and guidelines are going to continue to emerge from unexpected and unforeseen places, and not just the accounting standard setters that most market watchers are familiar with examining. How this will play out, however, is going to vary depending on how the various agencies that oversee U.S. financial markets overlap but will invariably influence how the asset class emerges and evolves.

One definite step in the direction toward clearer and more comparable regulation is the proposal put forward in February 2025 by Senator Bill Hagerty in the form of The GENIUS Act, which attempts to improve the reporting, disclosures, and auditing that exist around the stablecoin sector. An important note is that the primary focus of the Act seems to be two stablecoins in particular; USDC and USDT the two largest privately issued stablecoins as well as the two largest dollar-backed stablecoins in U.S markets. Several of the key points included within the GENIUS Act include, but are not limited to, the following:[1]

The *Guiding and Establishing National Innovation for U.S. Stablecoins (GENIUS) Act* is a bipartisan legislative proposal introduced in the U.S. Senate on February 4, 2025, by Senators Bill Hagerty, Tim Scott, Cynthia Lummis, and Kirsten Gillibrand. This act aims to establish a comprehensive regulatory framework for payment stablecoins – digital assets pegged to a fixed monetary value, typically the U.S. dollar. The GENIUS Act begins by clearly defining a payment stablecoin as a digital asset used for payment or settlement purposes that maintains a fixed value peg. It outlines licensing procedures for both bank and non-bank institutions seeking to issue stablecoins, ensuring equal access under uniform regulatory standards. A core requirement mandates that stablecoins be fully backed on a one-to-one basis by high-quality liquid assets such as U.S. dollars, Treasury bills, or other cash equivalents. To ensure value stability and consumer protection, the act prohibits the use of algorithmic mechanisms to maintain a stablecoin's peg, effectively banning algorithmic stablecoins. In terms of regulatory oversight, the act assigns responsibility based on issuer size: depository institutions with over $10 billion in market capitalization fall under

[1]https://www.whitefordlaw.com/news-events/client-alert-the-genius-act-a-compliance-roadmap-for-stablecoin-issuers-in-2025#:~:text=The%20GENIUS%20Act%20creates%20a,prioritize%20coin%20holders%20in%20bankruptcy

Federal Reserve supervision, while non-bank issuers of similar size are regulated by the Office of the Comptroller of the Currency. Smaller issuers may be regulated by state authorities, although a waiver process exists to allow issuers above the threshold to remain under state jurisdiction. Transparency is also a central focus, with issuers required to submit monthly reserve certifications conducted by registered public accounting firms. Falsification of information is subject to criminal penalties, reinforcing accountability and safeguarding consumer trust.[2]

The GENIUS Act Will Lead to Crypto Dollars

One of the most important discussions connected to tokenized assets and especially stablecoins is something that is outside of the crypto; how can the USA take effective action to maintain the reserve currency status of the U.S. dollar? The dollar has faced challenges to its geo-political dominance in the past, but few instances of these challenges have been combined with the shifting political landscape unfolding at the present. The European Union, partially due to increasingly strident language by the U.S. related to tariffs and NATO-affiliated defense spending, is looking to expand the use of the euro on a global basis. China, the second largest economy in the world and definitive rival to the USA, is expanding trade, infrastructure, and use of the yuan on a continuous basis. Lastly, the BRIC nations are actively seeking to develop and deploy a joint currency, which would seek to serve as an international medium of exchange.

The dollar's status as global reserve currency is not one that can be assumed to continue over the coming decades, and even less so in the face of technologies that are redefining payments and financial markets on a daily basis. The GENIUS Act represents an excellent first step toward codifying and regulation around dollar backed stablecoins, relegates non-dollar backed stablecoins to secondary status, and will improve the transparency with which these coins operate. As the dollar seeks to maintain its leading status on the global level the embracing of technologies to improve the efficiency and ease with which dollars can be used should be an imperative. Much like how the rise of the petro-dollar created a virtually endless demand for dollars, tethering the value to the paradigm shifting technology of tokenized payments will go a long way toward ensuring continued leadership.

The currencies and nations that embrace tokenization and blockchain-based payments will be the ones that assume and maintain leadership into the future; U.S. policymakers should continue to focus on integrating stablecoins and integrating blockchain to underpin the U.S. dollar.

The SEC

Under the leadership of past chairperson Gary Gensler, it could be said that the SEC worked hard to undermine and stall the development of the cryptoasset

---

[2]https://www.congress.gov/crs-product/IN12522#:~:text=The%20bill%20would%20establish%20rules,status%2C%20and%20using%20deceptive%20names

industry in the USA to a significant extent. These actions took the form of lawsuits, enforcement actions, and stonewalling attempts made by the private sector to develop and enact objective and pro-innovation regulations and rules. The end effect of these actions taken by the SEC was a stifling of innovation and growth of the U.S. cryptoasset sector, while at the same time allowing frauds such as the massive scandal that unfolded at FTX to occur in full sight of the U.S. investing marketplace. Following the re-election of Donald Trump, however, the actions and mindset at the SEC have undergone a complete pivot.

Acting chairperson Mary Uyeda took rapid and comprehensive action to redirect and reorient the SEC, highlighted by the establishment of a crypto task force – led by SEC Commissioner Hester Peirce – to develop frameworks and guiderails for institutions seeking to operate in U.S. markets. The confirmation of Paul Atkins to return to the SEC, this time as the head of the agency, and as a decidedly pro-crypto advocate, seems to highlight the pro-crypto position and pivot that the SEC will be taking moving forward. Commissioner Peirce is widely seen as pro-innovation and pro-crypto policymakers, and the establishment of the Crypto Task Force with her at the helm is widely seen as positive development for the sector at large. Specific actions that have been taken include, but not limited to, the following.

Since stepping into her role as head of the SEC's Crypto Task Force, Hester Peirce has been busy reshaping the landscape of cryptocurrency regulation. Her leadership marks a shift away from the SEC's historically heavy-handed approach of regulating through enforcement, opting instead for clarity, collaboration, and modernization of outdated rules. The Task Force was officially established in January 2025 under Acting SEC Chair Mark Uyeda, with Peirce at the helm – a natural choice given her reputation as "Crypto Mom" and her long-standing advocacy for sensible crypto policies.

One of the Task Force's first major moves was the rescission of Staff Accounting Bulletin 121, or SAB 121, which had required financial institutions to record client-held crypto as liabilities on their balance sheets. This rule had long been a thorn in the side of banks and exchanges, making it expensive and risky to custody crypto assets. With the SEC withdrawing the policy on January 23, Peirce signaled that her Task Force was willing to correct past overreach in order to better accommodate digital assets within financial institutions.

Just days later, Peirce delivered a public statement outlining the Task Force's priorities. Rather than enforcing vague rules that left the industry in a state of confusion, she promised a comprehensive framework that would give developers, exchanges, and investors clear guidance on what falls under the SEC's jurisdiction. She acknowledged that not every crypto project is a security and made it clear that the SEC needed to work harder to distinguish between those that are and those that aren't. Her team would explore regulatory exemptions for certain token offerings, refine how broker-dealers handle both crypto securities and non-securities, and provide much-needed clarity on issues like crypto lending and staking.

Peirce also highlighted the need for international collaboration, noting that the decentralized and global nature of crypto makes it impractical for the USA to go it alone. Her message wasn't just for the industry – it was for policymakers and regulators across the globe. She even encouraged public engagement, inviting feedback through written comments and meetings with industry players, a move that was a breath of fresh air for many who had felt ignored under previous leadership.

In early February, a more symbolic but equally important change occurred: the SEC reassigned Jorge Tenreiro, its top litigator who had spearheaded many high-profile cases against crypto companies. Tenreiro had been instrumental in lawsuits against major exchanges like Binance and Coinbase, but his departure from the enforcement side was seen as a nod to the new era Peirce was ushering in. The message was clear – litigation would no longer be the SEC's primary weapon in dealing with crypto.

Hester Peirce's actions thus far reflect her commitment to building a regulatory structure that promotes innovation while protecting investors. Her work has already sparked optimism in the crypto world, with many hoping her approach will bring long-term stability and encourage responsible growth in the space. In a world where crypto has often been seen as a regulatory minefield, Peirce seems determined to provide a map.

The OCC and Regulatory Changes: Implications for Crypto Payments

In order to achieve mainstream adoption and integration within the USA and other major marketplaces, a significant barrier that must be overcome is the barrier directly connected to normalizing crypto banking. Specifically, even though the banking industry is among the most highly regulated and controlled industries on the plan – and with good reason – the dialogue and open channels of communication between banking regulators, TradFi institutions, and the cryptoasset sector have been a long time in coming. Reasons for this sluggish pace can be attributed to any number of facts but include (1) the volatility that has long been closely associated with the crypto sector, even large and established tokens such as bitcoin, (2) the spectacular collapses and fraudulent activities that continue to occur on a recurring basis, and (3) the choice by the OCC and other banking regulators to ignore certain previously issued guidance and pronouncements that prescribed best practices for how U.S. banking could access the cryptoasset marketplace. Let's take a look at a few of the implications of how 2025 changes to OCC guidance have the potential to reshape the cryptoasset payment landscape.

First, the clarification issued on Article 1170 and new issuance of Article 1183 makes clear what the expectations for banking institutions seeking to offer trading, custody, and other banking services to crypto clients. In essence what these requirements are include the fact that same rigor and standard creation process that is used for developing standards for TradFi customers must be applied to crypto customers. Second, by explicitly acknowledging the prescribed guidance in Article 1170, the OCC has formally acknowledged the processes that need to be put in place to accomplish these outcomes the proverbial door has been opened to allow U.S. banks to move aggressively into this space.

U.S. banks offering cryptocurrency custody services is a big step toward bringing digital assets into the mainstream financial system. By providing secure storage, banks make crypto more accessible and trustworthy, especially for institutional investors who might have been hesitant due to security concerns. This move also signals growing acceptance from regulators, giving cautious investors more confidence to enter the market. With banks involved, we could see increased liquidity, less volatility, and smoother integration between traditional money and digital currencies.

However, there are challenges too. Regulatory uncertainty, cybersecurity risks, and potential conflicts with the decentralized nature of crypto raise important questions. While banks offering custody services can provide more security and oversight, it also means shifting control away from individuals and back to traditional financial institutions – something that goes against the original spirit of cryptocurrencies. Still, this development could pave the way for more financial innovations, like crypto-based lending, staking, and investment products. In the long run, banks getting involved in crypto custody may help shape the future of digital assets, making them more widely used and accepted.

No matter how the evolution of policies at the OCC evolves and develops the reality is that the landscape for cryptoasset banking and banking adjacent services are set to expand and develop over time. How this will play out is, of course, indeterminable at this time, but it is safe to say that the landscape and outlook for these developments is expanding, and that the regulatory environment for such developments looks continued to be positive moving forward.

AI Regulation

AN additional are in which the regulatory and policy landscape has been changing and evolving is in the realm of AI regulation as this industry has continued to grow at an accelerating pace, as well as attracting ever growing amounts of investment. In February 2025, the proposed bid for OpenAI – led by Elon Musk that nearly totaled $100 billion – illustrated how large this asset class and economic area had become. Although that specific bid was short-lived, it did highlight the growing competition around, interest in, and value of the AI sector for both the U.S. economy at the global economy.

The impact and implications of AI are still evolving and will need to be assessed as the economic and societal impact of these technologies continue to accelerate, but it does appear that the global AI conversation has separated out into three parallel development paths.

The first option is being put forward by the USA under President Trump, which highlights a hands-on approach to regulation and oversight, preferring to let the private sector and private sector actors take the lead on the development, marketing, and general proliferation of AI in the marketplace. A private sector approach mirrors the regular pathway that has led to the creation of world-leading firms in multiple industry areas. In the European Union, contrastingly, the approach has focused almost exclusively on regulation, oversight, and leading with compliance based initiatives to establish guardrails for firms operating in the space. Regulation and attempting to lead through regulation might be effective in well-established industries such as financial services but may stifle much-needed innovation required to develop AI further. Lastly, the Chinese mainland government has followed a well-worn path by seeking to nurture the AI sector via state-based agencies. Heavy state support for certain industries has assisted in the meteoric rise of the Chinese economy, but it remains to be seen if the fast-moving and nimble AI space will allow centrally planned success.

In the USA that has also been a flurry of executive, legislative, and state-level actions around AI, AI development, and how AI is implemented that include, but are not limited to, actions taken below.

Since 2024, the USA has taken some big steps toward making sure AI develops in a safe, fair, and responsible way. It started with an executive order signed by President Biden in October 2023, which set the tone for how AI should be handled across federal agencies. The goal was clear: manage the risks, ensure the technology is fair and equitable, and protect privacy. This was followed in 2024 by a national security memorandum that laid down rules for using AI in defense and security settings, with a strong emphasis on transparency and making sure AI doesn't lead to bias or unfair outcomes.

In early 2025, President Trump signed another executive order aimed at keeping the USA at the forefront of global AI innovation. It focused on using AI to drive growth and security while safeguarding human welfare. On the legislative side, Congress introduced the Generative AI Copyright Disclosure Act in 2024, which requires companies to be upfront about any copyrighted material they use to train their AI models. This is part of a growing effort to hold developers accountable for how they build these powerful systems. Another important bill, the No DeepSeek on Government Devices Act, passed in early 2025, banned a Chinese AI app from federal devices over concerns about data privacy and possible surveillance.

At the state level, Colorado led the way by passing legislation in 2024 that forces companies working on high-risk AI systems to take precautions against discrimination and provide clear, consumer-friendly disclosures. California also tried to push forward with the Safe and Secure Innovation for Frontier Artificial Intelligence Models Act, which would have required safety testing for advanced AI models and created a shared cloud resource for startups and researchers. However, that bill was vetoed by Governor Newsom in September 2024.

Altogether, these actions show how seriously the USA is taking the challenge of regulating AI. The government is trying to strike a balance between encouraging innovation and making sure the technology doesn't cause harm – whether that's in the form of biased algorithms, privacy violations, or national security risks. It's a fast-moving space, but the message is clear: AI needs guardrails, and those guardrails are starting to take shape.

The increasing amount of legislation and regulatory guidance also seems to indicate and provide an example for how the accounting and financial services industries will need to evolve moving forward. Specifically, the impact of automation and AI on the accounting profession is already being felt across industry lines, but the launching and codifying of rules and frameworks will only lead to more integration of both AI within existing industries and the reality that an increasing number of industry verticals will become overlapping as well as face growing integration moving forward.

A core takeaway from the continued development and refinement of AI policies in the USA is that these developments are partially in response to market forces such as the rise of multiple competing AL models as well as geo-political competition. Be it the much-hyped DeepSeek – which after an introductory splash has receded from mass marketplace conversation – or some other form of AI the implications are the same. No matter which specific tool is referenced the importance of comprehensive, logical, and well thought policies to help foster a supportive and innovative landscape for further AI development is imperative. Geo-politics are set to play a leading role in these conversations for better or worse, and the investing community should be aware of these realities as investment decisions and capital allocations are planned out.

ESG Policy Developments

While ESG has had a tumultuous relationship with the business and investing marketplace during the last several decades as it has continued to move to a more wholly integrated aspect of the business landscape, the reality is that the power of these trends is difficult to overstate. Even with the politization of ESG seemingly becoming the standard operating procedure for ESG in the modern business and investing marketplace, there are some trends that are going to redefine technology and business developments moving forward. Let's take a look at a few of them.

Increasing Power Consumption Will Drive ESG

Even as technologies such as AI and crypto continue to generate and create headlines with adoption, inventions, and other business applications, the fact is that all of these applications are increasingly power hungry. Crypto mining has been generating headlines with regard to the power necessary for years at this point, and while states such as Texas (pro-crypto adoption and usage) and New York (anti-crypto adoption and usage) have led the conversation, the industry has moved beyond state-specific issues. To put it simply as the crypto industry has become increasingly mainstream among TradFi institutions and retail users, the demand and power requirements for these applications will continue to increase. Even as bitcoin mining recedes to the background – with bitcoin being the only cryptoasset utilizing proof-of-work consensus methodology to any significant extent – the power demands for consensus protocols and the processing of crypto payments will necessitate the further expansion of power supplies.

AI is also driving an uptick in demand for electricity across the USA as well as in other areas, with Sam Altman spotted meeting with French President Emmanuel Macron in February 2025 during a major AI summit held in Paris. This is interesting for a number of geo-political reasons but one reason stands apart in terms of the potential impact it will have on the E in the ESG conversation going forward as it relates to the power conversation. France, unique to Europe and most industrialized nations across the world, generates a plurality of total power via atomic energy sources and actually generates more electricity than it usually needs in the majority of instances. OpenAI, co-founded and led by Altman, remains among the leading AI firms in the world, requiring ever larger amounts of electricity and power creation to power and maintain AI applications as they continue to advance.

Atomic energy is an area that has been somewhat controversial in the environmental landscape and environment going forward. Specifically, the aftermath of past nuclear disasters as well as the Fukishima meltdown in Japan has soured some policymakers and environmental groups. These concerns, although justified and completely understandable, overlook the reality that nuclear power is among – if not the – safest forms of electricity production in the world. As the number of AI applications and cryptoasset payment applications expand and accelerate going forward, it will be all the more important for all forms of electricity production to be on the proverbial table.

It is also worth noting that the continued development of AI within the power generation and distribution aspects of the economy will also assist in managing a grid that is both increasingly decentralized and under increasing strain. AI bots, blockchain-based applications, and the digitization of payments and trading activities at large all converge to increase the level of power demanded and consumed by enterprises. In coordination with the growing power generated via non-fossil fuel sources – solar, biomass, hydro-electric, and the like – there will be a growing expectation that the grid itself will become more volatile. This has already been seen in nations that – in an attempt to reallocate and proportion the power composition currently used – have pivoted away from less renewable but traditionally more steady sources of power such as atomic and natural gas.

With the ability to process, analyze, and redirect the sources and uses of power on an on-demand basis, AI-based applications and analytics have the real-world ability to enact change in a real-world basis and environment.[3]

---

[3]https://investingnews.com/brics-currency/

https://fxopen.com/blog/en/what-is-a-petrodollar-and-how-does-it-affect-the-global-economy/#:~:text=The%20Bretton%20Woods%20Agreement%2C%20established,searching%20for%20a%20new%20anchor

https://www.jdsupra.com/legalnews/sec-abandons-numerous-gensler-era-1441485/

https://kpmg.com/us/en/frv/reference-library/2025/sec-rescinds-sab-121.html

https://cointelegraph.com/news/sec-moves-top-lawyer-crypto-cop-jorge-tenreiro-wsj

https://www.gtlaw.com/en/insights/2025/5/federal-reserve-and-fdic-withdraw-crypto-asset-guidance-for-banks-occ-issues-clarification-for-banks#:~:text=Takeaways,tailored%20guidance%20in%20this%20space

https://www.reuters.com/technology/artificial-intelligence/openais-altman-says-musk-offer-is-tactic-to-try-mess-with-us-2025-02-11/

https://www.whitehouse.gov/presidential-actions/2025/01/removing-barriers-to-american-leadership-in-artificial-intelligence/

https://leg.colorado.gov/bills/sb24-205#:~:text=On%20and%20after%20February%201,provisions%20in%20the%20act%2C%20including

https://news.gatech.edu/news/2024/10/04/nuclear-energys-renaissance-thanks-ai-needs#:~:text=Meeting%20AI's%20Growing%20Energy%20Needs,push%20for%20sustainable%20energy%20solutions

Future Directions for Crypto and AI Financial Institutions

With the regulatory pivot that appears to be underway in both the USA and other financial markets, it remains to be seen how exactly these technological changes will drive change within the TradFi sector. Although different regulators, including both the OCC and FDIC, have published regulatory updates and changes to policy oriented to banking institutions, the effects of said changes will also be felt by the fast-growing fintech sector. Interestingly enough, it is important to note that Coinbase – still the only publicly traded crypto broker dealer – has enough assets under custody to rank among one of the largest banks in the USA. Let's take a look at a few of the changes that are set to arise as AI and on-chain assets continue to permeate the financial landscape.

1. Lower margins and consolidation. Following trends in other aspects and areas of the financial marketplace, the integration of more advanced technologies will almost inevitably lead to margin compression and increased competition for existing customers. Especially as one of the primary benefits of on-chain assets is the speed and lower cost of transactions, this will lead to customers looking to capture these benefits. As a result of these lower margins and increased competition, this will also lead to eventual consolidation across economic lines. Mirroring the trends that occurred following the Great Financial Crisis, it remains to be seen the appetite of regulators to allow further consolidation by TradFi firms. In essence, this could lead to the crypto sector undergoing a rapid consolidation while TradFi firms continue to expand operations and offerings.
2. Increased liquidity and volatility. Be it taking the form of AI-powered trading and algorithmic decision-making or other automated trading and payment processes powered by on-chain transactions, there are certainly upsides that are going to be captured by both the firms and customers alike. With the increased liquidity, however, there is also likely to more volatility due to higher speed with which trading and liquidity activities can be interjected within the marketplace.
3. Crypto-based payments will almost certainly become more commonplace as a result of these efforts by TradFi institutions to embrace the upsides and opportunities created by more crypto opportunities. Specifically, the likelihood of dollar-based stablecoins and stabletokens becoming mainstream will be assisted due to the simple fact that if consumers have access to dollar-based tokens via dollar-based banking partners the ease with which transactions can be conducted will also be increased. Ease, transparency, and the instantaneous nature of said transactions will all help create an ecosystem within which investors and users of cryptoassets will expand.

No matter what form the rise of crypto banking and payments takes, and even if the regulatory pivot currently underway has modifications or other changes in the future, the trend has been established. As nation-states, large institutional investors, and large enterprises alike seek exposure to the cryptoasset ecosystem, the demand for banking products and services will also increase. With TradFi moving into the space in significant way….

Action Steps for Financial Professionals

One of the most common questions, when financial professionals are confronted with a rapidly changing business landscape, is how exactly these changes should be prepared for and dealt with moving forward. After all, financial professionals are usually already tasked with juggling multiple demands and responsibilities as part of everyday responsibilities. Let's take a look at a few of the best practices that professionals can use to learn from, engage with, and deploy AI based solutions.

First, there will be an expectation and requirement of continuous learning and proactive engagement with emerging technologies that will need to permeate every level of the organization in question. This can include traditional educational opportunities and offerings, of course, but will also need to incorporate more non-traditional forms of education and learning. This can include taking certificate programs, organizing in-house trainings with outside experts, and also incorporating these trainings into pilot programs within the firm.

Second, the prevailing headset within financial services organizations will also need to evolve and change, even as these changes have been underway for decades. For a long time, the ideal has been for financial professionals to move from providing compliance-oriented services to offering forward looking services. In the modern era, and especially with the developments possible via AI and GenAI, these possibilities are closer to reality than ever before. That said, to maximize the benefits of such a pivot will also require a shift in the mindset of all individuals to one that is closer to a conservative risk taking process as opposed to the risk averse mindset so closely associated with the accounting profession.

Third, the fact remains that the influence of external factors on the accounting profession cannot be ignored. Specifically, the rise of PE firms and investors within the business landscape is already enacting dramatic changes on how firms operate, talent is hired and retained, and how new service lines are entered into. For example, there is at least one CPA firm – that after receiving PE money – has instructed certain employees at the firm to remove the CPA designation from email signatures, marketing materials, and even LinkedIn profiles. This is because the PE investors are actively restructuring the firm, how the firm operates, and has actually divided the actions of the firm and its employees into two separate and distinct areas.

Additionally, there is going to be a generalized restructuring of the accounting field in terms of opportunities, business lines, and the ability to attract and retain talent over time. How this plays out will obviously vary from firm to firm but involve several core items of similar nature.

Conclusions and Future Directions

The landscape for business technologies continues to develop and innovate on an almost continuous basis, and with every development and evolution of new technologies, there will be equally as dramatic changes for the professional services landscape. While the specifics are going to continue to need to respond to client demands, there will also be expectations that these service lines and opportunities embed technical features that are coming to market on a continuous basis. Moving from professionals focused on compliance or overly technical work to those more oriented toward strategic advisory services is – for the first time in mass market memory – something able to fulfilled in a realistic manner.

Printed and bound by CPI Group (UK) Ltd, Croydon, CR0 4YY

15/02/2026

14826293-0002